Reading Between The Lines

A Peek into the Secret World of a Palm Reader

Reading
Between
The Lines

A Peek into the Secret World
of a Palm Reader

Wendy Willow

BOOKS

Winchester, UK
Washington, USA

First published by O-Books, 2011
O-Books is an imprint of John Hunt Publishing Ltd., Laurel House, Station Approach,
Alresford, Hants, SO24 9JH, UK
office1@o-books.net
www.o-books.com

For distributor details and how to order please visit the 'Ordering' section on our website.

Text copyright: Wendy Willow 2010

ISBN: 978 1 84694 672 1

A CIP catalogue record for this book is available from the British Library.

Design: Stuart Davies

Printed in the UK by CPI Antony Rowe
Printed in the USA by Offset Paperback Mfrs, Inc

We operate a distinctive and ethical publishing philosophy in all
areas of our business, from our global network of authors to
production and worldwide distribution.

CONTENTS

To the memory of David John Nelligan, MD, a gentle healer
who left this earth too soon.
A more loving and devoted husband, soulmate and friend I
could never ask for.
Thank you for encouraging me to grow, to follow my dreams,
and to be myself.
Thank you for being there ...always.
Thank you for being there...
Thank you for being.

Introduction

Have you ever wondered what it's like to be a Palm Reader? Can they really see the future by looking at someone's hands? Or do they just make it up? Can they really look right inside someone and know everything about that person? Kind of gives you the shivers, doesn't it?

What are your thoughts and feelings about Palm Readers? Do you conjure up visions of wrinkled old ladies in long gypsy-like skirts? "Come into my tent, dearie, and I'll tell your fortune, for a handful of silver, of course!"

Ha! For me, nothing could be further from the truth. I just happen to be a Palm Reader; a very normal-looking woman, young in spirit, but apparently in my middle years, who loves to wear jeans and comfy T-shirts. I have no use for shoes as they restrict my feet. For that matter, I hate hats and bras too. A free spirit, that's what I am and I love reading people. As far back as I can remember, the charismatic pull of magic, the mantic arts; and yes, even the occult was as enticing as sweet, life-sustaining nectar to a hummingbird. Children are by nature inquisitive, opening the intuitive channel as easily as we in later years choose to block it, labeling it imagination, or relying instead on facts. And as a child, I was no exception; always wanting to know everything: what lay below the surface? What were people really thinking behind those polite masks? What was going to happen tomorrow, next week, next summer? What was inside a mountain? Who lived up in the clouds? Just what did lie beneath the ocean floor?

Was it Intuition that whispered to me our family picnic would be cancelled the following day? I almost said to my mother, as I watched her standing at the kitchen counter making sandwiches, "Why are you making lunch for our picnic, when we won't be going?" But I kept silent. The next morning, sure enough, one of my brothers had come down with a sore throat and a fever, so we stayed home.

How did I know that my teacher would hand out a test on any given school day? I didn't *always* know, but most of the time I had a premonition or funny feeling in my tummy. I was happy to write school tests 'way back then. They were easy, so it wasn't as if I was dreading these tests. Was Intuition at work here too?

How did I know that one hot summer afternoon at the lake my baby sister would nearly drown? One minute she was playing quietly in the sand and the next, she had toppled over, slipping under the water. Nobody saw her. I had wanted very badly to go and swim with my older brothers, but had this inexplicable feeling that I should stay close to my little sister. Fortunately, we were playing at the water's edge where it was shallow, so I grabbed her tender arm and yanked her up. Opening myself to the intuitive forces as a child, was as natural as breathing.

That open intuitive channel was to play a significant role all through my life. In my quest for hidden knowledge, with its roots in childhood, I didn't realize that intuition was the key, and that by developing it, I would find my pot of gold. I would find the means to uncover hidden truths. But it would take many years for those pearls of wisdom to be mine.

For hours, I would sit watching a magician perform, my eyes focused on his every move, so that *I* could be the one to discover his secrets (just how *did* he pull that famous rabbit out of his black top hat?)

The occult: that which is hidden, secret, not divulged, beyond human understanding – intrigued me, teased and tickled my brain, then danced away on a summer's breeze, out of reach during my busy child-bearing years. Cinderella's Fairy Godmother, The Magic Mirror in Snow White and the Seven Dwarfs, The Pot of Gold at Rainbow's End and The Sorcerer's Apprentice were all fuel for my inquiring mind. Imagination didn't even enter into it. In my childish heart, these stories were

2

all true.

I peeked into the bathroom mirror looking for the Wicked Witch, peddled my bicycle as far as I could go, bound and determined to follow that rainbow at all costs. I made a sorcerer's hat complete with glittery gold stars and sparkly crescent moons. And I tried; I really tried to turn Ginger, our marmalade cat into a horse, our Halloween pumpkin into a shiny new bicycle – all to no avail.

Time passed. I grew up and put all thoughts of divination, magic and rainbows away. What I didn't know was that those thoughts really didn't get very far: a little sparkle of curiosity that refused to go out, a flicker of a candle flame, a glowing ember, sat simmering on the back burner of my mind. Years passed and that simmering slowly ignited a fire; a fire that became passion, a passion that would push me into the realm of the "reader" back where I had begun. I had come full circle; from childish awe and wonder of the magician's sleight of hand, to the adult's belief in the mystical, intriguing powers of the mind; the explicit, yet often conflicting language of the body, and healing powers of the spirit.

My journey began at The Palmistry Centre in Montreal, Canada where I studied hand analysis, or Palm Reading. Equipped with this scientific knowledge, I grabbed any and every palm I could. It didn't take long before I noticed feelings and visions coming to me as I looked at peoples' hands. The intuition I had ignored for so long was beginning to stir and make itself known. It felt so good to read somebody accurately; to know where they used to live, to understand their work situation or what was happening in their relationships. They would look at me in wonder and exclaim, "How did you know?"

The more confidence I gained, the better my readings became. The more I trusted my intuition, the more information came through to me, which I then passed on to my clients.

Wow! This process was happening so fast, it was almost

overwhelming! I am just an ordinary, everyday person, doing laundry, shopping, and looking after my family - and Palm Reading or reading people, as I like to think of it. Some people think what I do is strange. I've been called a "flake" a time or two. Even my own parents chose to ignore this side of me, steering any and all conversations toward safer topics; like work, gardening or current affairs. Yet I assure you that I am genuine.

Originating in India approximately 4,500 years ago, palmistry (or chiromancy as it was first called), was used as a form of personality counseling or hand analysis, practiced strictly by the village medicine man or priest (who very often was the same person; there was no split between spirit and body back then). Checking a person's hands was one way of detecting illness or gleaning information about someone's health. Predicting the future was not part of hand analysis. There was nothing weird or deceitful about palmistry in those days; it was a common practice and very much accepted.

A Healer would typically start his consultation by studying the size and shape of his client's hands. Hand shape, or morphology reveals valuable information about the person extending those hands:

*A conic-shaped hand is wider at the base than the fingers; somewhat like an up-side-down ice cream cone. The fingers are long and smooth with tapered tips.

Conic hands belong to artistic people. Sensitive and passionate, they live to create beautiful surroundings. Ordinary rules and restrictions fly out the window, as they immerse themselves in worlds of their own imagination.

*People with square hands are just the opposite. Practical and down-to-earth, they *need* rules and structure to give them a framework for their daily lives. Farmers, teachers, caregivers and builders are members of the "square hands" club. Patient and persistent, they have the energy and nature to organize and carry out a job from start to finish. You can see why Ms. Conic Hands and Mr. Square Hands would have a hard time co-existing. They are both so different, and yet each has his own unique skills and abilities to contribute to our world.

*The psychic hand is long and slender. Fingers are long with knotty joints, making for deep analytical thinking. People with psychic hands are spiritual, mystical, idealistic and have a tendency towards fragile health. You won't catch them soiling their delicate hands by digging in the garden. They gladly leave that activity to their square-handed neighbors.

Finger length is also important when analyzing or reading a person's hand. Since fingers are the modes of expression, the length of one's fingers determines how slow or fast someone will take to respond to a given situation. Short-fingered people act quickly. They are impulsive by nature. Energy produced by thoughts, darts quickly up short fingers, especially if the fingers are smooth, with no lumpy joints to slow it down.

Conversely, people with long-fingers love to take their time. Cautious by nature, they prefer to think things through before taking action or making decisions. Energy traveling up these fingers moves at a slower pace. An example that springs to mind is one of a harp player, whose long, elegant fingers slowly and gracefully pluck the strings of her instrument. The music will flow if her fingers are smooth, but if she has knotty joints, it may take a little more time to process and express her compositions. Knotty joints serve as bumps or detours in the road, making it even longer for thoughts to be turned into action.

Palmistry has grown and evolved from the Shaman's ancient dwelling to our modern day universities. It is possible in this day and age to receive a degree in palmistry, not only in India, but here in Montreal, Canada as well.

My goal is to bring back this old authentic concept of palmistry through my writing. I feel as though someone or something is guiding me to shine a bright light on and revive these ancient beliefs, so they can once again become the accepted interpretation.

How is palmistry linked with the healing process? Well, the more you learn about your inner self, the better equipped you will be to identify your problem areas. Once you begin to understand yourself and your needs (or areas of concern), it will be easier for you to decide which path to take towards healing. In this light, palm reading can be considered the diagnostic aspect of healing, or a place to begin. As Louise Hay says in her book *Heal Your Body,*[1]"......*we must GO WITHIN to effect the healing."*

Through reading your palm, I become your guide, as we journey along the path of life. A competent guide is also a catalyst. Catalysts make changes. The information I convey to you is intended to make things happen or invoke changes in your life. Palmistry enables us to study who we really are, not who we imagine ourselves to be.

People from every walk of life come to me with all kinds of problems and questions, from relationship woes to career choices to financial queries. Most of the time the answers lie within the individual. They just need a little help or guidance in bringing them to the surface.

The purpose of this book is two-fold: to transform the current perception of Palm Reader as questionable fortune-teller, and to share my experiences with you. Let's blow away the dusty old cobwebs you may have stored in the back of your mind. That stereotyped vision of a gypsy Palm Reader needs to be replaced with a modern up-to-date version of what a psychic reader is all about; for it's the "psychic" part that gives you the true reading. The tools are secondary.

Some readers use tarot cards as their tool for readings. Others are drawn to rune stones, angel cards, auras, numerology, or good old tea leaves. It doesn't matter what the medium or tool is. What's important is to choose someone who you feel comfortable with; someone you can trust to give sound advice; someone who will listen as well as speak, for you don't want to pay for a lot of useless information.

Finally, I would like to invite you into my hearth and home. *Reading Between The Lines* is a true story of real people. People with problems, fears, hopes and dreams. People who have chosen to bare their souls, open their hands, and let me in. Their trust has kept me humble, taught me many lessons and brought wisdom to my soul. In sharing these experiences, I feel a need to pass along a little of that wisdom, so I may help others on their journey towards their own healing.

Shall we begin?

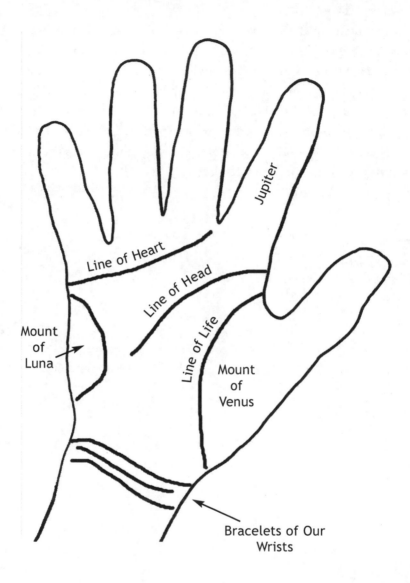

CHAPTER I

LIFE LINE LINGO

"Ooooohhh, my hand feels tingly!" exclaimed Valerie vigorously shaking her left hand, as if she wanted to shake it off.

"What's happening?"

Taken by surprise, I lurched forward in my chair and dropped her right hand – the one I had been engrossed in reading. Immediately I picked up the tingly one and focused my attention on her palm. An inflamed-looking patch of skin that hadn't been there a few minutes ago was growing on her Life Line.

"What's happening?" she repeated nervously, her eyes wide.

"Hmmmm!" I carefully responded, buying time.

Scented candles glowed softly, their flames picking up and intensifying the fear in Val's eyes. *Mountain Streams* played quietly in the background; the calming effect of rippling water providing a soothing atmosphere in my healing room. An atmosphere that had suddenly become thick, tense, almost chilly.

Val's reading had started out normally enough (if there is such a thing as normal). However, upon examining the Life Line in her left hand, I was alarmed to discover a definite break in the middle of it, as if her life was coming apart. Feeling instinctively that this broken line represented a delicate and possibly tragic situation, but not really knowing what it could be, I decided to wimp out. Hoping the answer would become evident as the reading progressed, I switched over to concentrate on her right hand.

That's when Val started shaking her left hand and complaining that she could feel "this weird tingling sensation". I was forced to pick up the troublesome left hand once again. It felt hot! Then I saw something strange. Right on that area where her Life Line was broken, an ominous-looking red patch of skin was beginning to form – just about the size of a quarter. This was obviously a signal for us to "pay attention". So, once again I focused on this area of her palm.

Never having seen this phenomenon before, I didn't answer immediately, but closed my eyes for a minute to "tune into" my favorite channel – the intuition frequency. Silently I sent out a prayer to the Universe "Please help me to interpret this situation properly. Help me to channel the right information for Valerie." In no time at all the message came through, strong and clear.

Val had come to see me to have her palm read. She was an attractive airline stewardess in her mid-twenties. Soft, amber-colored hair framed her face. Rather on the petite side, she sat before me in a bright blue chair, nervously crossing and uncrossing her slender legs.

"Val," I cautioned, opening my eyes so I could focus on her face. "Please be a little more careful over the next two weeks. Make sure your doors are locked at night. Look both ways before crossing the street, you know, that kind of thing?" I was trying to be as tactful as I could, not to frighten her, yet the warning had come through loud and clear. Whatever dreadful situation was heading her way, Val needed to understand that it was serious enough to attract our attention by manifesting as a red, tingling area of her palm. Shrugging it off would be the worst thing she could do.

"Isn't that funny," she said thoughtfully, her blue eyes showing more bemusement than fear. "My astrologer told me the same thing just two days ago. Thank you for the advice, I really will be careful."

"Thank you Universe," I whispered to myself, with genuine relief.

I never heard from Val again. That's the hard part. Some people come into my life once – only once. I have no idea what happens to them afterward. I just hope that Valerie decided to heed my advice and take extra precautions to protect herself. I wasn't able to nail down the exact threat to Val's safety. The message had come through as a feeling that pervaded my body, a shivery dark feeling of fear. All I could do was to send her healing white light and let go. Let go of control, and trust that whatever happens is meant to happen. I send all my clients on their way with a beam of white light for protection. It's my way of saying "thank you" for trusting me with your inner world.

Val's problem was in her Line of Life, one of the three major lines clearly seen in our palms. The Life Line begins about midway between the index finger (Jupiter finger) and the thumb, curves downward and ends somewhere on the "bracelets of our wrist". Take a moment to sneak a peek at your wrists. You can clearly see horizontal lines running from one side to the other, just like bracelets!

The other two major or predominant lines are: Line of Heart and Line of Head. These important lines define the expression of our thought patterns and emotions, as well as being the channels or circuits through which energy flows. Major lines represent *subconscious* patterns of thought and minor lines represent *conscious* thought patterns. Each line has a specific purpose or area of expertise.

The job of our Life Line, as it journeys down our palm, is to impart valuable information concerning our quality of life. It functions as our own natural barometer. Are we living our lives to the fullest with vitality and energy, or half-heartedly in fear? The deeper the line, the more a person jumps into life and enjoys it. Here you will find your deep-sea-diver, mountain climber, astronaut and film-maker – to name a few.

If someone has a rather faint line, they tend to be cautious and a little afraid of life. Risk taking is to be avoided at all costs. They will tend to stick with the same job or profession throughout life. Feeling safe is crucial and the faint-lined person will compromise new experiences and adventures for the sake of staying with what they know. Of course, it is important to understand that a Palm Reader must correlate his or her findings with whatever is going on in the rest of the hand. Breaks, islands, or dots on the Life Line spell trouble. Your palmist will be able to interpret these negative signs and pass the information on to you.

Jacoba, a heavyset European woman in her sixties had strong, generous hands. Her Life Line became weak and wavy in the area that corresponded to about 70 years of age. After that, it resumed its normal, strong, clear path. I told her that she would experience an unsettling illness, possibly a stroke within the next 5 or 6 years. Knowing that this kind of news would naturally upset her, I advised her not to become overly discouraged, because she would fully recover and live a normal life span (as evidenced by her Life Line resuming its clear path).

The weak period in her life was destined to force her family into a situation where they would be looking after her, rather than she looking after them. Her whole life had been devoted to the needs of her husband and seven children, with rarely time for herself. And now, even though her husband was retired and her children grown, she continued her over-mothering pattern of looking after everybody.

Unfortunately, the only way for her emotional needs to be acknowledged was through her own body giving in to dis-ease. For Jacoba it was time to change. Time to turn the tables so she would be in the position to *receive* care rather than *be* the caregiver. Because of this situation, her family would learn to appreciate her, rather than taking her for granted.

Some people are very concerned with the length of their Life Line. Perhaps because of misinformation, (those pesky cobwebs I mentioned earlier), they feel that if their Life Line is short, they will live a short life. Sounds logical. However, having a short Life Line does not necessarily mean that you will have a short life. It may mean that you are just not in the habit of making long term plans.

If you follow the curve of your Life Line to a point where it stops, breaks, then starts up again, you are in for a period of struggle or soul searching. This "interrupted" Life Line frequently means a total change in lifestyle or a move to a different country. It could mean an accident. A good Palm Reader will be able to tune into that area and interpret the information with the correct timing for her particular client. Being prepared allows you to change the experience or accept what lies ahead.

A short Life Line that does *not* resume later on usually means that the person does not think long-term, but enjoys life in a spontaneous fashion. Planning ahead is not their style.

Specific markings on your Life Line tell their own story. For example, if you see a little circle, like an island on your Line of Life, this means that you are headed for a temporary period of uncertainty or confusion. When will this likely happen? A good question – timing is everything. When will I win the lottery, find happiness, have children, change careers? How can a palmist give you an accurate time frame? The location, or where this circle appears on your Line of Life, is how we estimate timing. Of course, zooming in intuitively is the most accurate instrument I have.

Now, just because you have an island taking up residence on your Life Line, doesn't mean it's a "bad sign". Not at all. Sometimes we find ourselves stuck in a rut, and need to be shaken up a little. Confusion means change is just around the corner. The old comfy ways no longer fit, but we are unsure or unaware or afraid of the new, so we find ourselves in a confused state of mind. Knowing what lies ahead (as we peek into the future) is to your advantage. You can now prepare yourself to meet this challenge.

The sweep of the Life Line is important. When it is full and rounded with a good Venus mount (fleshy portion at the base of your thumb), we have a person who is bursting with life, full of ideas, plans and energy. Good-natured and lovable, they laugh and dance their way through life. Graceful is the way in which they handle life's challenges. And, they have an answer for everything.

A narrow curve of the Life Line belongs to someone who restricts him/herself and takes life too seriously. Theirs is a more conservative approach. Travel is risky and they live more or less status quo. If you decide to give a party and invite one of those "narrow curves", you will be disappointed, as they believe partying is frivolous and a waste of time.

Double Life Lines mean double trouble. No, just kidding. They mean double strength; a sign that will guide us towards finding and contacting our guardian angel (more about this in Chapter 6). These double or auxiliary Life Lines do provide us with an extra boost of energy or protection when we need it most.

Simon came to see me for a consultation. He zoomed in on a cherry red chair and promptly sat down, leaning forward. I estimated his age to be about 19 or 20. Stylishly and expensively dressed, he did not look like your typical college kid. A beautiful smile lit up his face as he looked at me expectantly.

He had absolutely no idea what he wanted to do with his life. A perfectly normal state of mind in a young person, wouldn't you say? So, naturally the length of his Life Line was short, reflecting his inner feelings. Not concerned in the least with the length of his Life Line, he was looking for direction. Reaching out for guidance, he needed help in unearthing his talents, his capabilities, in order to choose an appropriate career. His Jupiter finger (index finger) exuded strength; his Head Line dipped delightfully into the imaginative depths of Luna. Empathy towards others lay dormant in the texture of his hands, a quality that would come to life a few years down the road. I suggested to him that he become a schoolteacher or social worker. Simon looked a little disappointed, but thoughtful. To his way of thinking, these careers were not very exciting.

Years later, Simon contacted me to ask if one of his students could come in for a consultation.

"Certainly," I replied, pleased to find out that he had become a teacher after all. "So, Simon," I probed. "How do you like being a teacher?"

"You know," he answered. "At first I wasn't too thrilled with the idea of teaching, but after a while it started to feel right, and now I'm glad I made that decision."

"So am I," I smiled into the phone.

An elderly client came to me and jokingly said, "I have such short Life Line, how come I still leeve?" Luba was of Polish descent, carefully dressed with a traditional upswept hairstyle. Her demeanor spoke more of curiosity than of fear. Picking up her heavily lined, wise old hands, I saw immediately that indeed her Life Line was short. It stopped somewhere around age 40, but here she was sitting in front of me (on a bright yellow chair) full of life. After feeling into her energy, my intuition whispered to me that she was a person who lived life to the fullest, one day at a time. I told her so.

"Zat is correct," she replied slowly nodding her head. "But it vas not alvays so." Luba went on to explain that she suffered tremendously when her husband, her life long partner, died suddenly. It took her a long while to get over the grief that comes with losing a loved one. Once over the initial shock, and terrible pain, however, she began to think.

Sitting in her neighbor's kitchen one sunny afternoon in early spring, sipping fragrant cranberry tea, Luba suddenly felt something shift inside of her. A decision had to be made. Her tears had long since dried up, but she was still holding on to her pain. She could either be miserable for the rest of her life, mourning her loss, or she could grab life by the horns and live it to the fullest; however long that may be.

She shifted in her chair, eyes instinctively drawn to the open kitchen window and beyond, where the first signs of spring were making themselves known in Alma's garden. New life was beginning to stir; trees and bushes were bursting with fresh green buds, brightly colored crocuses peeked out from their hiding places in the rock garden, sunny yellow daffodils decided it was time to come to life.

"Wake-up!" they trumpeted to sleepy tulips, encouraging them to open to the sunlight and show off their palette of fresh colors. As if hearing the daffodil's call, vivid orange, yellow, red and pink blossoms opened up to catch the gentle breezes, as they wove their way into the tapestry of Alma's garden.

A curious chipmunk poked its nose out from under the woodpile, just in time to watch a pair of boisterous young squirrels tumbling about in the grass before scrambling up the nearest tree. Hustle-bustle, scurrying, humming – joyful sounds of activity signaling a time of renewal, wafted through the window to greet Luba's ears. Robins and blue jays flew in and out of vision, calling to one another and chirping out the news.

As Luba inhaled the fresh, clean smells and sounds of a brand-new season, a sense of hope swept over her. Face tilted to absorb the sun's warm, golden, healing rays, and feeling her close friend's genuine concern and care enveloping her, she resolutely made up her mind. Jumping to her feet Luba startled her friend who had just poured them both another steaming cup of tea.

"I've decided!

"Vot?" inquired Alma cautiously, setting down the teapot.

"I've decided to leeve each day like it vas my last. Life is precious gift to be enjoyed. Never mind tomorrow. Tomorrow may never come, then vot? But today I vill LEEVE!"

Mentally, she had been living her life one day at a time, and this was reflected in the length of her Life Line.

Your Life Line, whether long or short, is more an indication of how you embrace life, rather than a measure of how long you will live. As you walk along the path of life, the choices and decisions you make are reflected in your Line of Life. Each twist and turn, bump and pothole, flower and thorn you encounter along the way, is placed there for a reason. You decide what to do with each experience as you shape your life. It's your life. Live it!

CHAPTER 2

LET'S GET TO THE HEART OF THE MATTER

Do you ever wonder whether your palmist is telling you the truth? How does she know? Where is this information coming from? In palmistry, there are two elements that go hand in hand. Science and intuition. Like apple pie and ice cream; you can't have one without the other.

Opposite forces are what make up the creative process: male/female, yin/yang, day/night, concrete/abstract, science/intuition. Individually, they present a strong, yet one-sided power. Each can stand on its own. Science, or bare facts or mathematics on its own is fine, yet combined with intuition, creativity, wisdom, art, create an enriched, multidimensional force. What was good, fine, strong on its own becomes fabulous, exciting and powerful, when combined to create a new energy, a magical blend.

The scientific study of hand size, shape, lines and signs, can be learned, but the intuitive process is instinctive. You can't pin it down, lock it up or entice it to come out. Sometimes it flows like a sparkling waterfall; other times it behaves like a spoilt child and no matter how much you coax it, it just won't appease you. That fickle flow of intuition can also be affected by:

* The reader's feelings that particular day. Is she energetic and ready to work? Is she tired, wishing to be at home reading a book? Is something significant going on in her life just now?
* The client's state of mind. Is he excited, open and looking forward to the reading? Or closed, worried about receiving bad news?

* The room itself. Is the energy dark and heavy, light and airy, or neutral? Is it cluttered, sterile, or warm and inviting? There are times when I read in other peoples' homes, where I have little control over the reading area, so I bring my candle, some healing energy, and make the best of it.

By painstakingly reading only the lines of the hand, without the added gentle art of intuition, a reading will fall flat. Let's clarify this a little, shall we? Hand analysis teaches us that a break in your Heart Line, for example represents an interruption, a break, a separation. Without the interpretative part of the reading, how are you to know what that broken line means? A broken heart? Relationship? Heart attack? Or just a switching of loyalties?

A crooked baby finger belongs to someone with arthritis, right? Not always. Reasons for crooked fingers are many, physical and emotional. Each finger expresses a different quality. Your baby finger (*aka* Mercury finger) expresses how well you communicate. So, a crooked communication finger means you manipulate the truth? That is one interpretation, but it could also mean a temporary detour in your writing career. In other words, you are momentarily having trouble expressing yourself through the written word. Or, you could be the kind of person who takes things to the extreme, communicating to the world in an eccentric fashion.

Can you see how vital the art of intuition is when reading people? A valuable, accurate reading (one that is meant to make positive changes) is created by the winning combination - science of hand analysis, and art of intuition.

When I begin a reading, I like to start by first picking up your hand and feeling into your energy. Intuition begins flowing like an open channel once I touch your palm. In fact, some people refer to this process as channeling. Channeling information from the Universe. Information that I am meant to pass on to you.

Pictures flow into my stream of consciousness and I vibrate

with feelings you are sending me. An overall feeling or sense of you as a person begins to take shape in my heart and mind, frequently corresponding to your aura. Gradually, I begin to understand why you have come to see me.

Surprisingly, there are people who are closed, and don't really want a reading, so they repress or stop these feelings from flowing outward. Body language says it all as they sit back in their chairs, not really sure whether they should jump up and run away, or stay put. Reluctantly they extend their hands, fingers partially closing to form a nest, as if carrying a fragile baby bird.

The next step in the process is to concentrate on the lines in your palm – your personal map. Slowly at first, information about you flows into my consciousness, becoming the interpretive part of the reading. This interpretation is solely intuitive; a sharpened sixth sense and a real "knowing" of certain events, past, present, and future.

Once this interpretive channel is open, pictures, words, and even sounds flow so swiftly that I have trouble getting the words out fast enough. At times it can be overwhelming, swooshing over me like a tidal wave. Then, all of a sudden it is gone, and bang! I hit a wall. The intuition stream (or channeled information) has stopped.... has deserted me. Now what do I do with this wall? Do I go through it? Climb over it? Knock it down? How do I get around it?

After pausing for a minute to catch my breath, I pick up your hand again and start over. Gently, carefully, I begin to feel your energy once more and the door slowly swings open. Stretched out in front of me are many, many roads or pathways, each passage ending with another closed door. Wonderful! Now I am caught in a maze! Which path do we investigate first? Which door do we try? Which area is most important to you or which needs the most attention....now!? This is where I need *your* guidance. I encourage you to ask questions.

This is your time, your reading. Listen to your inner voice –

your own intuition, and allow your concerns to come out. Once we select a door and open it a crack, the process will have begun. Then like a hidden spring of water, the intuitive information will come pouring out once again and the next door will swing open, and the next and the next.

Questions are encouraged, for they are doorways to your inner world. If you think I know *everything* on your mind – you're wrong. I would not be human, if I knew your *every* area of concern. More than likely, I'd be burned at the stake!

Feedback is also important, so I know you are getting the right messages and understand what I am conveying to you. Words and phrases can be misinterpreted with unintended consequences. And sometimes, yes sometimes, I do go down the wrong trail. Without a signpost from you, I end up taking a wrong turn and give you information intended for someone else. How does that happen? I really don't know. All I can tell you is that if something doesn't sound right, speak up! Then we can turn around and start over.

What Is This Intuition Anyway?

How do you describe intuition? Psychicness? Channeling? Sixth Sense? For me, it's really an inner knowing, a feeling, a mental picture or a series of pictures. If the feeling is very strong, then I know beyond a shadow of a doubt that whatever I'm feeling or sensing is absolutely true. There is nothing mysterious about it. Just think about the times when you get "gut feelings". It's the same thing, only stronger. Everyone gets these "gut feelings" from time to time. If you listen to them, trusting that they are accurate, these feelings will become stronger over time. Ignoring them will only chase them away.

It was early summer of 1977. I was sitting in the park watching my two little ones playing in the sandbox. There was nothing special about that particular day. All around me children were playing happily or squabbling over toys as children do. I was alone on the wooden bench for the moment, totally relaxed and enjoying a little bit of precious solitude. I knew that before long, a friend, or a child's mother would walk over to join me for a chat over a thermos of coffee. Not that they would be unwelcome; far from it. But at that moment, I gave in to temptation and closed my eyes to rest just a little. Summer sunshine caressed my skin and I inhaled the sweetness of freshly cut grass. Sounds faded away as I relaxed.

Out of nowhere, a strange feeling spread over me like a vibration or a wave or a wake-up call. Immediately a picture flashed into my mind. I "saw" myself cradling a little baby boy in my arms. I knew instantly that I would have another child and he would be a boy.

At that point in time, I already had a 6-year-old son and a 3-year-old daughter. I felt that my family was complete. Having another child had not even crossed my mind. Before the birth of my other children I had not received any messages, so why was I sent this information over the intuition airwaves on this child who hadn't even been conceived yet? I don't know. Maybe I will at some point, but on that sunny, warm summer day, I just knew that he was coming into our lives within the year. That was years ago. The Wheel of Life turns, another generation is born, and Sean himself is a father.

Frequently, I am asked questions concerning family members or relationships:

"Is there someone out there waiting for me?"

"Will my boyfriend and I get married?"

"Can you tell me if my daughter will be successful in her career?"

"Will my father's health improve?"

Questions about others may or may not influence your palm, but the answers do come from the psychic or intuitive channels. I need to touch a specific area of your hand, while focusing on your question. Other Palm Readers have their own methods, but personally, I need to use touch as my entrance to the intuitive world. When a strong feeling comes over the intuitive frequency, I will then have the answer for you. By listening to my inner voice, I am guided to say what you need to hear wherever you may be on your path.

If that means telling you something to invoke a change in your life, then that is what I am meant to say, even if it is not what you want to hear. My role is one of a catalyst, helping you to make changes, giving you that little "push" out of your comfy, safe, familiar place.

There are times when someone asks me a question, to which I have no answer. Strangely enough, no feelings or answers come through to me. I just feel empty space.

It used to scare me at first. Can you imagine picking up a ringing telephone to answer it, and hearing silence? Nobody there. Or, imagine turning on a radio or the TV and…. nothing happens. I used to feel that there was something wrong with *me*. I was broken. I couldn't read anymore. Instant panic!

After a while though, I began to realize that the information was purposely blocked. There were specific reasons why I was not meant to answer certain questions. Perhaps that particular client had issues to work through on his own. An answer from me would probably influence his decision, and rob him of a valuable growth and/or decision-making experience.

Throughout life, we find many paths spread out in front of us, many different roads to take. Our choices are what shape us, give us strength, and teach us who we are. A Palm Reader acts as a Sage, pointing out upcoming pitfalls and helping to unearth inner resources; strengths and qualities that we may not even be aware of. As we discover more about our inner world, awareness gradually creeps into our consciousness, like an early morning sunrise sweeping the Earth with light. This new awareness brings us to another level, giving the encouragement we need to face our challenges and grow.

Rosa, a gentle, pleasingly plump woman in her early 50's was concerned about her relationship. "My husband and I are having problems in our marriage. Will we stay together or not?"

After looking at her Heart Line, my answer to her was "No, the two of you are not communicating openly with each other and if you continue on in the same pattern, you will not stay together." This is the information that came to me over the intuition frequency. It may not have been what she wanted to hear, but that is what came through loud and clear.

Rosa went home feeling a little uneasy. Her thoughts were churning around in her head and the more she thought about it, the more she wanted to reach out to her husband and make changes in their relationship (I learned later at another reading). She wanted to rekindle those feelings of love and intimacy that had somehow gotten lost along the way. Her plan was to open up her heart and share her thoughts and feelings with her husband. She was determined to communicate in a more positive manner, rather than always finding fault. Guiseppe, sensing the change in her, responded to her needs and wishes and happily, they decided to stay together.

Rosa had the courage to take charge of her life. She wanted to turn her life around and as a result, did change her future. In choosing to accept the challenge that lay before her, she was able to change her path.

I don't always know what people do with the information I pass on to them, but the intention is to unlock a door or trigger something within, so they will go ahead and make the necessary changes in their lives. This is the real intention or purpose behind my words, even if it is done intuitively, psychically, or by channeling. I do not consciously tell people what to do with their lives. I just help them to visualize what may happen if they continue on in the same old comfortable pattern, instead of moving on.

So if you need some help over a troubled spot in your life, or if you just want some reassurance that there is light at the end of the tunnel, then you take what I tell you and do what feels right for you. I cannot emphasize that enough. Do what feels right for you.

* * *

What about the lines on our palms. Can they really change? How is that possible? Incredible as it may seem, the lines on our palms really do change. Our hand, being a reflection of ourselves, changes when we do. If we change our thoughts, then we change our attitudes. Once we change our attitudes, our habits change. When our habits have changed, our lines change as well. Get it? I didn't think so.

OK, you think you aren't creative. Somewhere along the way someone (parent, teacher, sibling) told you you were no good at painting or drawing or dancing. So, you believed it. Your Head Line is short, and so are your attempts at creativity.

Then, suppose you write a poem, or discover you have a singing voice, or sketch a tree that actually looks like a tree. Wow! You really did something "creative". Encouraged, you try something else and something else. Before you know it, your attitudes have changed. You are receptive enough at this point to try all kinds of creative activities and enjoy them.

Now of course your habits have changed. You finally believe you are a creative person and, naturally, your Head Line has grown along with your confidence in yourself. You've broken a pattern and changed your lines. Knowing that your lines can change further lends credibility to the belief that you can exert some control over your future. Nothing is carved in stone, not even the lines in our palms.

[2]*"If we think of the brain as a computer and of the hands as the printer, lines and signs reflect a constant print-out monitoring our different modes of existence. For whatever shift occurs in the conscious,*

subconscious, or superconscious mind, the lines will alter according to these impulses."

So, if your lines change and what you tell me today may change next month or year, why bother? Because it's fun and entertaining? Exciting and interesting? Perhaps, but if you are genuinely looking for guidance, palm reading is a wonderful place to get started. It is also a wonderful way to get to know yourself. And it is empowering to think that you have some mastery over your life. Knowing you *can* avoid a potential disaster, or fix a problem gives you a measure of control, taking you out of the "helpless" spiral.

Once you've made the decision to have your palm read, you are ready to take that first step towards self- awareness, that first step towards finding the right path, the right connection linking you with whatever healing is appropriate for you.

Just by choosing to read this book, you have already set the stage. Perhaps you feel it is time to listen to your inner nudgings - those persistent little voices that refuse to be ignored. Maybe you feel out of balance somehow, blocked or stagnant. Listen to your feelings, for they won't lead you astray. You will know when the time is right. Time to learn all you can about your inner being. Time to pick up a book, go to a seminar, indulge in a personal reading.

It's exciting to think that once you go for your reading, the experience will be like finding hidden treasure. The key resides within your very hands; the key that will unlock your secrets. You may not even be aware that these old conflicts or blocks to happiness exist. They are cleverly disguised as procrastination, low self-esteem, ego or old behavior programming; which is why we need to bring them out into the open.

Once we've unearthed those elusive inner issues and brought them to light (sometimes this takes more than one reading), we are ready now to embark on our healing journey. Generally at this point, you will feel a sense of relief mixed with a little anxiety.

For some people energy balancing in the form of therapeutic touch, or Reiki is all the healing necessary to get back on track. For others, a change in diet will make a dramatic difference in the way they feel, particularly their level of energy (try giving up sugar or coffee for a week and see how you feel!). Spiritual psychotherapy, creative visualization, yoga, massage therapy, shiatsu, Tai Chi, utilizing herbs and homeopathic remedies are just a few of many options available to provide our bodies and souls with the healing we need. A little detective work is what it takes to uncover the right healing mode for you.

Whatever you choose, it is important to start the process of unlocking the energy blocks. Let go of emotional baggage clouding your aura, so once again you can allow the river of life to flow naturally, bringing feelings of joy and vitality back into your soul.

As mentioned before, bringing your area of difficulty or concern into sharper focus is the first step towards positive transformation or finding a solution to an area of your life that needs attention. Ignoring these pesky problems will only exacerbate them. They won't just dissolve or dry up and blow away, now matter how much you wish they would; but will remain just under the surface, treading water, until you force them to come up for air.

With the help of a sincere and intuitive palmist, however, you will have an opportunity to bring your problems to light where they can be explored and talked about out in the open. Positive energy, or a different point of view can be used to turn your situation around and make way for changes to happen (more about that later). Change is good. Why cling to old ways or patterns when they no longer serve any useful purpose, and in fact, keep you stagnant?

Even though lines change and what I tell you today may change over the following months or years, isn't it better for you, for your personal growth, to move towards pleasure and away from pain? In other words to change what is not working in your life: to go through the process, face the fear of change and come out a stronger, more powerful person, better equipped to handle the next set of circumstances life throws at you?

Suppose I foresee a financial loss heading your way, in your place of business. Rather than being upset, look upon this bit of "bad news" as a gift – the gift of insight. Now you can prepare yourself accordingly, bring your attention to the problem areas(s) and with a bit of luck, turn the situation around.

Giacciamo plopped his ample, round bottom into a yellow chair. He told me he had no problems at all, but was coming just out of curiosity. Ha! My sensors picked up something quite different Underneath that mask of bravado, was a man who was bewildered. Giacciamo owned a retail clothing business. Over the past few years, his company had been suffering financially, and he could not pinpoint the problem. He needed to come to a decision about whether to close down, or make drastic changes and try to go on. Looking at his rather large, meaty palms, I could see his Finance Line (more on finances in Chapter 7) was rather disjointed, as if someone had taken a pair of scissors and cut it up.

"How old are you?" I inquired suddenly. Giacciamo stared at me in surprise. "I'll be 51 next month, why?"

"You have another two business opportunities coming into your life over the next 10 or 11 months. One of them is just a test. Don't take it. The people approaching you are unscrupulous."

"How will I know?" he asked, concern sharpening his tone of voice. Ignoring his question for the moment, I continued. "But the other opportunity will be very lucrative. Take this one. It will be worth waiting for."

"But how will I know which one to take?" he pushed, growing impatient with me, his false mask slipping away.

"Your present business is not going well and is not likely to improve," I told him candidly, locking my eyes with his. He held my gaze, but said nothing, waiting for me to go on. "The sooner you close down the better," I continued, watching for a reaction.

A mixture of relief and sadness flashing briefly in his eyes told me that I had gotten through to him. He shifted to look out the window, as if looking for solace in the trees.

"Follow your instincts, follow your gut feelings," I advised. "You chose to sit in a yellow chair – the color of the solar plexus chakra, where your gut feelings originate. You will know when the opportunities are in front of you, which one to trust and which one to reject. Learn to trust yourself and your business decisions will become easier to make."

An interesting way to look at predictions for the future is to visualize them as tiny seeds. Will you allow these seeds to grow to fruition or atrophy and die? Let's take the example of you wanting a prediction for your financial state of affairs. "Will I win the lottery?" you ask. What if I say, "Yes, I see a winning in the near future."

"Well if that's the case, I'll just sit back and not bother to work hard at anything! After all, money is coming my way, so why break my neck?"

Work and productivity don't seem to be as important any more. You slow down. Your brain becomes lazy. Months seem to float by and somehow you even forget to buy your lottery tickets. Everyone in your little world seems to be in that passive, not-much-is-happening mode.

Years go by and it dawns on you that maybe you won't win the lottery after all. "What's happening?" you wonder.

So, back you come for a consultation. "What's going on?" you accuse. "You told me I would win the lottery." Looking into your hand once more I can see that you have changed. You are no longer the alert, positive go-getter you once were. As a result, your Finance Line has shortened. There are no expected lottery winnings. You have changed. Your lines have changed and your future has changed as a result.

Thinking that the prediction will happen all by itself doesn't always work. Remember, you are in the driver's seat. Take control of your life. You have been handed a gift, a seed to be planted. Do you want to water it and care for it so it can bear fruit, or leave it alone to waste away?

If on the other hand (no pun intended), you decide to allow my prediction of winning the lottery to increase your awareness, your energy, which in turn raises your vibration; you are co-creating your way to success. Put your best foot forward, sharpen your brain and skills and become receptive to wealth and happiness.

Perhaps with the idea of winning the lottery planted firmly in your head, you decide to start a pool in your workplace. Your enthusiasm and positive energy catches fire and spreads to your co-workers. They decide to have fun and go for it! Guess what? One of your shared tickets turns out to be a winner! You win because your elevated energy level positively influences your co-workers and you all win the lottery. Sounds too good to be true? It's amazing to discover how much control you do have over life's circumstances. Just by focusing on the positive, you attract more positive experiences to you. Your decision to nurture that little seed and reap the rewards, turned out to be a fruitful one.

So, I can give you a prediction, but it is up to you to take this information and do what is right for you. I can help you find the golden key, but it is up to you to unlock the door!

Sometimes the information I pass on to you may not make sense at that particular moment. Perhaps you have forgotten or blocked out an important experience from the past. Maybe you are not tuned in to or appreciative of certain qualities within yourself, or cannot even imagine glorious accomplishments still to come. Plans and goals can be made with the best of intentions, but do we really know what life has in store for us? I just might see you racing exotic sports cars, becoming an elephant trainer, or giving birth to triplets! If what I suggest takes you completely by surprise and you say to yourself, "Yeah, right!" just remember to keep an open mind.

People who never thought they had the dexterity to enjoy cabinet-making or woodcarving, might find themselves enrolling in a woodworking course at some point in their lives. Someone who was told by a parent or sibling that they had no ear for music, could turn out to be an amazing saxophone player, drawing enthralled crowds of people at the local nightclub. And we've all heard heart-warming stories of men and women who despite a serious handicap or disease successfully turned their lives around, to walk or run a marathon. Imagine what they would have thought of me had I even hinted at such a physically demanding achievement a few years down the road?

Some of the information you hear from me will be stored in your memory until you are receptive and the timing is right. Not everything can be consciously absorbed, but subconsciously you will have taken everything in, stored it and will call upon it when ready.

Logan's experience illustrates this. Early in the New Year, this serious-looking, overly responsible young fellow came to see me because he couldn't understand his girlfriend's behavior. Part of this misunderstanding stemmed from the family dynamics in his home. As I gave my full attention to the relationship area of his palm, a picture flashed across my mind. It was Logan walking into a bookstore, stomping snow from his shoes, while blowing on his icy fingers to warm them. I knew in an instant that I was seeing him a year from now. He would be seeking answers on how to cope with his dysfunctional family, by looking in the self-help section for an appropriate book.

I told him of my quick glimpse into the future. He gave me a funny look, but didn't comment. I went on to tell him I didn't know which book would be suitable for him, so I couldn't recommend anything. It didn't matter in any case, as I watched (in my mind's eye) him being led by his own intuition to a specific section in this bookstore. After about 10 minutes or so of scanning the shelves, he reached up to grasp a book.

Now, I am quite sure my prediction wasn't on his mind the rest of the year. More than likely, he forgot about it once he left my healing space, since his main concern was girlfriend problems. However, seasons change as they will. Spring melted into summer, summer danced into fall, and once again winter was upon us, crisp and cold. It was on one of these cold, snowy days, that Logan found himself standing in front of this same bookshelf in his favorite book store. Something tugged at his memory, and with an "ah ha!" he zeroed in on what I can only surmise was the right book for him Almost a year had gone by since I'd given him that tidbit of information, which somehow had been stored in his memory. Once the timing was right for Logan, the book serendipitously appeared.

There are as many different opinions and viewpoints as there are people. Some people try to test me by turning my questions posed to them, back to me. For example, someone came to my booth for a reading at an Alternative Health Fair. I sensed a void within him that I felt intuitively was because he had no children.

"Do you have any children?" I asked gently.

"You should know, you tell me!" he shot back by way of an answer. Because for some people this might be a sensitive issue, I chose to ask him, rather than stating bluntly "You do not have Children's Lines in your palm and I'm picking up an emptiness in you, which feels to me like regret over not having children." That kind of approach immediately makes a person feel uncomfortable; not my intention and certainly not the way to begin a reading. Of course not everyone wants children, and many are fulfilled without little ones.

Other people will ask questions such as "Let's see how good you are – what happened to me on June 1, 1988?" This line of questioning serves no useful purpose. Information and intuition do not always come forth on command. When I am being tested, I feel that the person is more interested in trying to find mistakes in how I work, rather than in healing or discovering themselves. On the other hand, if they would have said, for example, "I feel pain whenever I think back to my preschool days. What do you think it could be?" This indicates a genuine concern for a problem, which has probably been blocked out over the years. I absolutely invite these questions and concerns, and yes, I will tap into that time frame intuitively, meanwhile looking for significant markings on that particular area of your palm. This is how we begin the process – the process of unlocking those doors or energy blocks within you.

Like anything else in this wonderful world of ours, the more you invest in something, the more you will get out of it. Palm reading is no exception. The more receptive and open you are, the more energy will flow spontaneously during a reading, and the more you will benefit.

Obviously, I do not "click" with everyone. Quite a few years ago, a woman came to my booth at the Psychic Fair in Montreal, Canada. Everything about her was rigid and closed. She sat down abruptly, pulled out her money, crossed her legs and thrust her hands in my face. From then on it was downhill all the way. I could feel her resistance to what I was saying. Even though she had come to me for a reading, she was not ready to face herself openly and honestly. Her true self was buried; her mask too tight. Nor was she prepared to admit that something was clearly bothering her, right down to the core of her being. She had made a decision concerning an important relationship and was looking to me for confirmation. She hoped I would agree with her and make her guilt go away.

However, her palm clearly told another story, so I could not confirm her decision. She had chosen to harden her heart and shut her sister out of her life for good. Her Heart Line was long and sensitive, so I knew her decision must have been done impulsively, at the height of an argument or something of that nature. Now, it is not my place to make judgments – people are free to make their own choices and decisions, of course. My "transgression" was telling her something she did not want to hear, which made her angry. I told her that her sister would very soon be back in her life again – this time for good. She stood up in a huff and demanded her money back.

Believe it or not, there are people who are geared to hear only doom and gloom. If I tell them something positive, they don't believe it. It is as though they are walking under a thundercloud, not able to see or experience the wonderful, warm sunshine, as it struggles to poke its way through the heaviness.

"In your dreams!" Bernie responded when I told him he would be going on a world cruise. "Just open your mind to the possibility, feel it, dream it, and then draw it towards you," I counseled. "That is," I laughed trying to lighten the mood. "If you really want to go!"

Interestingly enough, people react in different ways when I tell them something that is "right on". Some are frightened and exclaim, "How did you know that?" As a result they close down and don't want to be read. Others are thrilled, open right up and thirst for more and more and more.

Some people come for a reading looking for answers to specific questions. Others feel that they are at the bottom of a pit with no way out. Their lives are a total chaos. They feel lost and alone. Coming to me is a last resort. I prefer to look at it as "taking the first step" rather than nowhere else to go.

Even if you feel lost or hopeless, seeking help is a step – that first step on the path to healing, enlightenment or just change. People who resist change have a hard time to grow. What they don't realize is that change is inevitable. It is a natural part of life, like a river flowing to the sea.

Let go and allow yourself to flow and you will be far less stressed than if you rigidly refuse normal, healthy change.

Gaby came to see me for a reading. I had seen her several times over the years. Unfortunately, her marriage had broken up six months previously and it looked as though her printing shop was failing as well. Stringy dark hair hung over her face. She was depressed and it showed. Shapeless black pants and baggy sweater hung from her anorexic body. She wore no make-up or jewelry. A very distinct smell (bluntly put: body odor) tickled my nose, so I leaned forward in my chair to casually light the tip of an incense stick with the flame of my candle. Then I began her reading.

Cautiously, she extended her hand to me while turning her head away and squeezing her eyes shut. "No more bad news!" she implored. "Please tell me something good!"

"Well", I began, after taking a few minutes to make an assessment. "I do see some interesting things." I was deliberately not giving anything away.

"Oh no, here it comes," she uttered somewhat apprehensively, while shrinking into her chair.

Treading softly I continued "It looks as though there have been some uncomfortable changes relating to your printing shop." She stole a peek at me through the curtain of hair covering her face. "Tell me something I don't know," she muttered, rolling her eyes.

"Either your customer base has changed, or the neighborhood has become more competitive or totally different. The surrounding energies have transformed into something that doesn't support the shop like it once did. It is time to let go." I suspected a lot had to do with Gaby's own personal energy, which at this point in time was attracting darkness and failure, rather than success – but wisely held my tongue.

I waited a minute for her to absorb this news. "Now," I went on, "if you can adjust your thinking to acknowledge that the print shop was part of your old life, and put it behind you, we'll move on to some good news."

"Which is?" she asked sitting up a little straighter in her chair. "I see some good possibilities for you to consider."

"Oh, like what?" Gaby cocked her head to one side, like a little bird ready to listen and gave me an inquisitive look.

"How about catering? With your nurturing hand, strong thumb, and creative Head Line, catering would come easily to you. Or," I went on, "I can see that you are a patient person who would understand and work well with the elderly."

"No, I don't want to work in a nursing home!" she interjected, sounding anything *but* patient. Laughing, I continued. "How about teaching seniors to improve their driving skills? I know there are many retired folks whose driving skills have deteriorated, due to vision or other health problems. They've lost confidence in themselves and feel they are losing their independence. With a little retraining and practice, these people could once again become active members of the community, instead of depending on others for their transportation."

I could see that she needed a little time to think this information over, so I decided to take a few minutes and add up her date of birth.

"Let's see if your numbers support these new business ventures. When were you born, Gaby?"

"September 6, 1969."

"When I add up each digit in your date of birth (9+6+1+9+6+9=40), it becomes a 40. Again, you add the digits together until they become a single number (4 + 0 = 4). Your date of birth adds up to a 4.

The number 4 belongs to someone who builds foundations, someone who is stable and trustworthy. The stability of 4 is represented by four corners of the earth, four seasons, four elements (air, earth, fire and water). Because you are working a 4 vibration in this lifetime, you are constantly building (whether at work or play) and you are an excellent organizer to boot! Your method of accomplishment is always in a step-by-step manner. I can see why you were drawn to printing in the first place. But now it is time to change. With your good business sense and experience, you will have no trouble starting up a new venture. Take some time to think about what would bring you the most happiness and go for it! I believe you could become very successful."

Somewhat relieved, but thoughtful, Gaby left. "I'll be back!" she called out merrily over her shoulder, and walked right into the closet.

Numerology – the vibration of you

I often blend numerology into my palm readings for additional insight. What exactly is numerology? Numerology, or the science of numbers, is a method of character analysis as old as time. Down through the ages, man has been fascinated by the power of numbers. Pythagoras, a famous Greek mathematician living approximately 600 B.C. believed that life was based on numerical patterns. He viewed the human soul as immortal and taught how our life paths dance to the tune of a certain frequency – the frequency or vibration of our birth date. Each of us is unique. We are born on a specific date and time; energies released on that very day characterize each one of us as an individual. The numbers of our birth date guide us to learn important lessons and help us fulfill our mission in life.

How do we find your birth path or destiny? You simply add up your date of birth, as we did with Gaby.

For example, someone with a birth path of 1 may not be aware of their leadership qualities. The number 1 carries the vibration of a trailblazer, a leader, a pathfinder. The birth path of a 1 is one of originality and creativity; an initiator, a beginner, a catalyst. As a child they might have been reprimanded for always wanting to be first, when this is their very nature – to lead the way.

A person with a number 2 vibration is born to be supportive of others. It makes sense when you think about it. Number 1 is the leader; number 2 the balance or help person. Gentle by nature, imaginative and romantic, they prefer to follow and harmonize, keeping the peace. Needing to feel needed, they succeed much better when working behind the scenes, rather than right up on stage.

Someone coming into this world as a 3 is here to learn to express themselves freely in a creative way. The number 3 is the number of the family, the triple goddess, the holy trinity, a cycle of completion – mother, father and child. A child born with a 3 vibration should be encouraged to seek all avenues of creative expression.

Heather was born on March 20, 1978. She will add up each digit (3+2+0+1+9+7+8=30). Next, she adds together the resulting number, which is 30 (3+0=3). Heather's birth path or destiny number is a 3. So if Heather works her 3 vibration in the positive – she will feel balanced, happy and loving, as a designer, musician, writer, graphic artist or painter.

Gaby on the previous page is working the number 4 vibration in this life. Four corners, four walls, a perfect square. In a favorable light, this is viewed as practical; negatively, it sounds boring. As they plod along through life, the patience of a 4 will strengthen the practical, and redeem the boring.

Do you know someone adventurous? Someone spontaneous who will pick up and travel at the drop of a hat? That someone is your typical 5. A person who jumps into life with enthusiasm and boundless energy. Communication is their birth path, languages their forte. Charismatic and popular, they are fun to be with.

Number 6, the teacher. Their birth path is to educate with patience and love. Sympathetic and supportive, they easily respond to social needs of others, while balancing unfairness and inequality. If you happen to be a 6, then marriage and domestic harmony rule. Your home reflects your feelings as well as your deep appreciation of the arts.

The number 7 is a sacred and magic number, used in many

societies for mystical ceremonies. In the bible, the seventh son of the seventh son was said to be special, blessed with charm and clairvoyance. Lessons in this life are to search for the truth, study, meditate, but be careful of losing touch with reality. Healers, philosophers, and dreamers all resonate with the number 7.

Power and abundance best describes the life cycle of a number 8. To be successful in the material world is their passion. Because of their strong individuality, physical drive and intense nature, those walking the 8 birth path are chosen to command positions of authority and power. Ancient belief has it that the figure eight represents the joining of the two spheres of heaven and earth.

Nine is the greatest of all primary numbers because it contains the qualities of all the others. It reproduces the creative power of three and signifies completion of a cycle. The birth path of a 9 is one of healing, counseling and philanthropy. Drawn to metaphysical studies, their wisdom comes from delving deeply into the well of their many past lives. Someone born with a 9 vibration is a sage, leading others towards the light.

Your birthday is your key. If you understand the meaning of your numbers, you will be able to channel this ancient knowledge to guide you successfully throughout life.

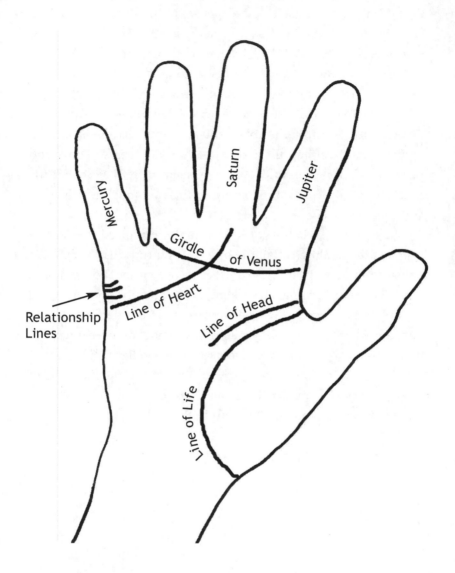

CHAPTER 3

HEALING THE HEART LINE

We talked about the Life Line in Chapter 1 as one of the three major lines on the palm – the conscious lines of expression. The Heart Line is another important line, located in the upper part of your palm closest to the base of your fingers. It begins at the edge of your palm under your baby finger (Mercury) and slowly arches upward to end somewhere between your Jupiter (index) and Saturn (middle) fingers. This innocent little line tells us all about your love life. If you think you can hide the truth from your Heart Line – think again! It will snitch on you every time. Your emotions and how you handle them are also written into the code of your Heart Line.

As previously mentioned, the Life Line will tell us about your vitality and life energy, while the Heart Line speaks to us about your emotional nature and expressions of love.

A long Heart Line that reaches out towards the Jupiter finger belongs to a person who has a great capacity to give and receive love. Devoted and supportive, they make excellent marriage partners. If this long, sensual Heart Line is graced with a fork at the end, you will have a sensitive soul who gives love freely.

Someone who is cooler and less emotional in matters of the heart will have a shorter Heart Line. Makes sense, doesn't it?

Intersecting lines that seem to slash through the Heart Line indicate broken love affairs, disappointments or betrayals. Everyone goes through heartache, but how you handle it is important for your emotional well-being and your growth.

Nothing is worse than a broken heart. To feel rejected by someone we love is to feel wounded, severed, bleeding – seeping deep down to the roots of our very soul. What's worse is to be left in the lurch, while our sweetheart merrily rides off into the sunset with someone else. When we have been hurt or rejected and our heart has been broken, we instinctively withdraw, or build a wall of protection around us in an effort to avoid going through the pain again. "Next time I will be more careful," we vow to ourselves.

However, if we can go through the pain, accept that which we cannot change, (we cannot make someone love us nor can we make people behave the way we want them to) and focus on the growth and experience which are to be gained, we will be quicker to get back on our feet, ready to face the world again with new eyes, a little wiser.

One thing to remember is that the two of you were together for a reason. Relationships are an essential part of life, mirroring our inner beings. We grow through our relationships, as we learn to see ourselves with more clarity. If it is time to move on, know in your heart that the next person will come into your life when you are ready, and the new relationship will be stronger.

Georges came to see me and sat in a black chair, his aura a cloudy gray. His movements were nervous; eyes darting here and there like a hunted animal. I sensed his discomfort and remained quiet and centered, waiting for him to begin.

"What can I do?" pleaded Georges, the sadness of his soul overflowing into his deep brown eyes. "If you follow your heart, you will never go wrong," I counseled, soothingly.

"But you don't understand," he replied impatiently, shaking his head. "My honor is at stake here." I didn't think anyone thought that way anymore – especially one so young.

Oh boy! I thought to myself, quickly scanning his person: impeccably dressed and rigid. Rigid in body, rigid in mind. Probably religious or strict upbringing. To his way of thinking, outward appearances mean everything. Whoa! These guys are the toughest people to get through to.

A hard-working young fellow of Greek origin, Georges was in

trouble. He told me he had been dating a lovely young lady for the past three years. At this point in time, the young lady in question and her family were waiting for and expecting a proposal of marriage. Georges felt trapped. I had a funny feeling that he was in love with someone else, but was too embarrassed to admit it.

"If you marry someone you don't love," I advised, "your relationship will only get worse. Your wife will feel your unhappiness and lack of devotion and become unhappy too. Then what? Instead of honoring her, you will be cheating her out of a loving marriage – to which you are both entitled. You will be doing the opposite of what you intended in the first place."

"I think she might be pregnant," he sighed, in a convoluted attempt to hold on to this "honor issue". Intuitively I knew that this was not true.

"Look Georges," I said gently. "I'm not here to judge your actions or tell you what to do with your life. I'm only your guide. It's up to you to do what you feel is right. Keep that in mind – do what feels right for you."

Looking at his palm, I noticed that his Heart Line was long and curved upward towards his Jupiter finger. This sensitive Heart Line belonged to a sensitive man. A Girdle of Venus, which looked like a half circle or a beautiful smile, ran just underneath his middle 3 fingers. Another sign of someone who cares so much for others that he sometimes forgets himself.

"Your hand shows me that you are a very caring man, capable of a loving marriage someday. I see Children's Lines on your palm as well, although not for a while. Try to break free of that rigid pattern you were taught as a child and turn some of that caring inward towards yourself. I know that's not how you were brought up. You were taught to look out for others first. If you always look out for others first, who is looking out for you?

"Perhaps, however," I added thoughtfully, "that is your pattern of Family Karma. We evolve through living within the framework of family patterns or karma, particularly in the area of relationships. Some of these patterns are meant to be broken or released. For example, the role of women being subservient to men; or in your case, honoring others before yourself. The hard part is that if you don't break that pattern now, you will create another set of circumstances to accomplish this lesson. The same situation will come up again and again until you finally break that pattern and replace it with self love."

I took my finger and began gently, but firmly rubbing the lines running transversely at the base of his left thumb.

"Georges, whenever you think of it, rub these Family Karmic Lines with your finger, like this," I instructed. "This is called "Palm Therapy" and will help you to break the Family Karmic pattern."

I didn't see or hear from Georges again. I suspect he chose not to take my advice and married the young lady anyway.

How can palmistry help you to find a suitable partner, a lover, a soulmate? We will begin by understanding you - your feelings, your reactions, your expectations. Remember, your emotional experiences are all encoded in your Heart Line. What kinds of experiences are shaping your future? Were you brought up in a loving environment, or was your early life full of pain and fear?

Exploring your past will reveal your early life patterns of behavior, your expectations of people, and ultimately the reasons behind your reactions in certain situations. In short, what kinds of experiences have molded you? Do you constantly seek out the same personality types only to be hurt time and time again? Are you the one who is always left behind, or are you the one to break up? What's going on inside you?

Your Heart Line gives an accurate picture of the manner in which you express your love. For example, if you have a very short Heart Line, more than likely you are afraid of being involved in a love relationship. Fear stems from the belief that love is painful. Relationships can be tricky, full of misunderstandings and expectations. Consequently, short Heart-Lined people will keep their feelings tightly controlled, rather than risk open expression and possible rejection. They prefer to erect walls around their feelings, so they can hide safely.

If you have a branch of your Heart Line that reaches down towards your Head Line, it's a sign that you'd rather love with your head; meaning that you tend to rationalize your feelings because it's easier and less painful. By choosing to stay in your head, you cop out in the feeling department. Thinking your way through situations, rather than feeling is how you protect yourself. Your head rules your heart, so your heart doesn't get broken.

Some of us will choose to stay that way for a good long time, but others will open their hearts and trust their feelings when the time is right. Once they decide to risk feeling their emotions again, their Heart Line will grow, curving back up where it belongs. With Head and Heart Lines back in balance once more, harmony reins and, they will love with their heart and think with their head – the way it's meant to be.

For people with short Heart Lines, it would be preferable to find a partner who has a long, open, forked Heart Line; someone who is able to love unconditionally, who will give the care and support needed by the person with the short Heart Line. In this relationship, the person with the short Heart Line will feel loved and supported, allowing the walls of protection around the heart to crumble. The resulting feeling of trust will be reflected back to the person with the long, sensitive Heart Line for an enduring and happy relationship.

Check this out – two people with short Heart Lines *finally* get together. Does it work or not? You guessed it – each person is afraid to trust the other. Each person gives "a little" love and then waits to see what will happen. If their expectations are not met – suspicion instantly rears its ugly head. Trust erodes and so does the relationship. Fear blots out the sunshine and the once beautiful love fades away. Suspicion replaces trust, as both hearts remain closed in fear. When fear closes the heart, the flow of love stops.

Will these two ever find happiness together? Only if they are willing to override their suspicion and make a conscious effort to change. If they are willing to face their issues of trust and learn to overcome their fear, their lines will change and so will their relationship. In practical terms, this means open and honest communication. Talking out their feelings (no matter how silly or irrational these feelings may sound), will help each person understand the other.

Harry was confused. His wife didn't understand him, didn't love him, he thought. He worked very hard every day, often not coming home until late. Saturdays would find him back on the job – a construction site. There was not much time for enjoying their relationship.

"I don't know what's wrong with her – I give her everything," he fumed.

"Maybe the problem is not with her – it's with you." I suggested in a neutral tone of voice.

As you've probably figured out – Harry's Heart Line was short. He had trouble expressing his love. So when his wife started to feel "shut out", and withdrew her affection, Harry withdrew even more and stopped trusting their relationship altogether.

Relationship Lines or marriage lines also help to determine whether a person is truly able to make a commitment. Relationship Lines are found on the side of the palm, the part of your hand you would use to demonstrate a karate chop. They appear just underneath the little finger.

If someone has many Relationship Lines, then you know that that person has a hard time making a commitment. They will be bopping in and out of relationships wondering why they can't seem to settle down, especially if their Heart Line also has many "feathered" lines at the end.

A truly committed Relationship Line looks clear and straight, with no drooping or forking at the end. If someone interferes, or breaks up a marriage, the Relationship Line forks, the new line of the fork indicating the other lover. You can see that the fork in a Relationship Line means something entirely different than the fork in the Heart Line. In the Heart Line it denotes a sensitive soul; in the Relationship Line another lover can be the cause of major upset, with feelings of betrayal all around. And in the Head Line, if you have a fork at the end, we call this a Writer's Fork – a good sign if writing is your passion (but we're getting ahead of ourselves – chapter 5 deals with your Head Line).

A relationship line that is long and droops or curves downward, signals a Karmic relationship. The partners have shared a significant relationship in a past life, and are working on issues that weren't adequately dealt with previously. Although the attraction is mesmerizing in the beginning, challenges soon spring to the surface. How one goes about dealing with these challenges determines the outcome of the relationship.

A short drooping relationship line tells of a short, painful marriage. For reasons known only to themselves, this couple unwisely chose marriage. Motives for this are as varied as there are people: escape from an intolerable situation, financial security, social reasons, etc. Unfortunately, this kind of union is doomed from the start.

Are you working through Family Karma in the form of relationship problems? Sometimes the unresolved past will surface, wanting attention like a small child. If you ignore it, it won't go away, but will keep coming back until you deal with it. When these relationship problems surface, they are there to be worked through in order to break old negative family patterns.

Isobel, a factory worker, attracts men into her life who have problems with addiction. Her father, an alcoholic, taught Isobel that he was the important person in the household. Isobel learned to ignore her own needs, so she could tend to the demands of her father. Placating her father was done out of fear, for he had a wicked temper. Isobel's mother was no help, for it was she who had set the example of giving in to him right from the start. Isobel never learned to effectively deal with this demeaning pattern.

Instead, she moved out of the house. A year or so down the road however, Isobel fell in love and married a wonderful man. Once she found out he was addicted to alcohol, Isobel was devastated. After a few years of giving in to all of his needs, she left him. Her next husband turned out to be an addict as well. Through her tears, she begged me to give her some good news. She wanted me to tell her that she would eventually find a wonderful man who did NOT have an addictive personality.

"Isobel," I said to her. "You do have another Relationship Line, but you must learn to look after yourself and not continually "give in" to the demands of your partner. Your needs must be met too. You must learn to love yourself and do what is right for you. Compromising yourself because someone else has an addiction or is weak-willed, will not help either of you. The sooner you break this pattern (for that's all it is) the better for you. Repressing or ignoring yourself and your needs for the sake of another is draining and will leave you vulnerable. You won't have the energy or inner resources to stand on your own two feet and live independently.

And it looks as though you have developed an unhealthy need to be needed. I suggest you take some time to be alone for a while and learn to value yourself just the way you are. When you come to a place within your soul where you feel centered and complete, it will be time to find a partner.

Don't forget the Universal Law of Attraction. Like attracts like. If you are needy and dependent (as you are now), then that is exactly what you will attract in a man. Support yourself and become more independent and you will attract a man of like qualities."

Smiling through her tears, Isobel thanked me and left. About a year later, I heard from Isobel again. She hadn't found a partner yet, but (much to my surprise) wasn't overly concerned with her situation. She had decided to leave the factory, upgrade her education, and had just been accepted into a program of study to become an art therapist. She sounded happy and was looking forward to the challenge of a new career. I was a little concerned over her choice of career, but didn't give voice to my feelings. I was wondering if becoming a therapist was perpetuating her karma instead of changing it.

Sometimes all it takes is some happy news; a flicker of hope that a romance is near, to bring back that sparkle in your eye, that soft glow in your aura which will encourage someone special to dance into your life.

If on the contrary, it appears that no one is in sight in the near future, that usually means you still have internal work to do before you can join energy fields with someone new to make a couple. The more you can clear away old emotional debris from your energy field, the lighter you will become. When you raise your vibration in this way, the more highly evolved person you will attract. He or she will be worth waiting for!

The Universe did not intend for us to be alone. We were made to love and be loved; to find a partner, lover, soulmate and create – a male energy to balance our female and a female energy to balance the male. A palmistry consultation can help you find that special someone – someone to share the joys of a happy, loving relationship, which we all deserve.

Colors and Chakras

By this time you must be wondering why I always mention the color of the chair that each client chooses to sit on. What is the significance of these different colors? Each color corresponds to a specific chakra. According to Eastern philosophy, chakras are whirling funnels of energy found in the physical body. The seven major chakras are located at specific points along our spine. They absorb universal energy (i.e. chi, prana), process it and then send it through the nervous system to specific endocrine glands. Each chakra is associated with an endocrine gland and a particular area of the body. The chakras also have psychological and emotional implications.

When my client chooses to sit on a red chair, for example, he probably has some survival issues to work through, since **red** is the color of the first or **root chakra**. The root chakra (wouldn't you know) is located at the base of your spine – your tailbone.

Besides survival issues, other psychological or emotional issues associated with the root chakra are: fear of being threatened by the external world, fear of feeling unsupported and alone, stagnant anger.

The endocrine glands that the root chakra feeds are the adrenals. The areas of the body governed are: the spinal column and organs of elimination.

Orange, the second chakra or **sacral chakra,** represents creativity and/or sexuality. Its location is just under your belly-button. Lively, energetic people are usually drawn to an orange chair. Of course, people with blocks in this area, who aren't so lively also choose this color, because they need the zest of orange to pull them out of the doldrums.

Issues surrounding this chakra are: excessive or blocked creativity, sexual expression or identity, abuse, victim mentality.

The associated endocrine glands are the gonads. Areas of the body governed are the kidneys and reproductive organs.

Yellow is the color of the **solar plexus chakra**. We all know where our solar plexus can be found (yes, right in our gut, or stomach if you prefer).

Issues concerning personal identity are usually associated with this third major chakra. Self-esteem, fear of rejection, intellectual insecurity, fear of responsibility and apathy are also team players in the emotional make-up of this chakra.

The endocrine gland concerned is the pancreas, and areas of the body governed are: stomach, liver, gallbladder, nervous system. Have you ever given any thought as to why your "gut feelings" originate in your gut? Our solar plexus is really a specialized major network of nerves. It is these nerves that pick up extrasensory feelings, so are appropriately named "gut feelings".

Pink or **green** are colors of the fourth chakra – the **heart chakra**, located where else? In the center of your chest where your heart lives. Obviously, the focus is on loving and nurturing.

Issues of nurturing, compassion, empathy, relationships, resentments are all covered in the heart chakra.

The endocrine gland at work here is the thymus. Body parts are heart and blood, vagus nerve and immune system.

The fifth major chakra, the **throat chakra**, is **sky blue** in color. Now sky blue is a lovely, serene color, but people who have trouble expressing themselves often sit in a blue chair.

Speaking your truth and expressing your creativity are issues of the throat chakra. If you are afraid to express your emotional needs, feelings or opinions, then you are also creating blocks in your energy field – walls to hide your true essence behind.

The thyroid gland is associated with this chakra, and vocal cords, lungs and the alimentary canal are the areas of the body nourished. So, if you have a sore throat, what do you think it means?

The sixth chakra or **"third eye"** smack in the middle of your forehead, is a **deep indigo** color.

Intuition, clairvoyance and headaches are associated here. Psychic abilities, fear of looking inside oneself and anxiety resonate with this sixth chakra.

The pertinent endocrine gland is the pituitary and areas in the body are: lower brain, ears, nose, vision and nervous system.

The **crown chakra** or spiritual chakra (the seventh and last) is a point about 6 inches above the crown of your head. The color is either **pure white**, or **violet**.

Acceptance of life and path, courage and faith in oneself and the universe, spiritual crisis, negative behavioral patterns that result from unwillingness to grow and change, are some important issues or challenges of this chakra.

The endocrine gland associated with the spiritual chakra is the pineal, which is located in the brain. Immune system and upper brain are the areas in the body governed by this chakra. Do you know anyone who always wears purple? Most likely, they are trying to connect with spirit and feel good wearing purple or violet. Or, they are already very spiritual in nature and feel in tune with these colors.

Do people always choose a color to go with their issues? No, some people sit anywhere, not even noticing the colors. Yet, I still find it interesting to see which of the colors clients are drawn to, for most of the time they unknowingly give themselves away.

So let's backtrack. Val in Chapter 1 sat in a bright blue chair, the color of the throat chakra. This tells us her issue on that day, appeared to be communicative in nature. There was nothing else to suggest that Val was unable to "speak her truth" or express herself in her daily life, but a very strong issue of communication (actually a warning) screaming at us through the "hot spot" on her palm turned out to be the focus of her reading.

I think Simon's choice of red chair had more to do with his strong and youthful energy level at that time than any problem in his root charka. Survival issues and/or fear did not appear to be a concern for him.

Luba was totally tied up in her inner being, her self identity. She had a hard time coming to terms with her husband's death, letting go and moving on with her life. Choosing to sit in a yellow chair, the colour of the solar plexus chakra gave me a clue where her reading would be headed.

Giacciamo from Chapter 2 also chose a yellow chair. His solar plexus issues had more to deal with learning to trust his "gut feelings" than issues of personal identity.

CHAPTER 4

OPENING THAT FORBIDDEN DOORWAY – THE PAST

Sounds ominous, doesn't it? A forbidden doorway leading..... where? There are times when bits and pieces of your past flash across my intuitive screen. Some people do not want to know anything at all about what happened earlier on in their lives, and some people do. If my intuition is sending me information about your past, then there is a reason for it. Sometimes accessing the experiences of childhood or adolescence turns out to be a valuable source of information for us. Awareness is always the first step. Once we become aware of past experiences, circumstances or decisions made, we begin to understand why difficult issues or situations keep popping up, or return to haunt us.

What lessons have we still not learned? By looking into the past we develop a greater understanding as to what has shaped and/or scarred us, why we behave the way we do today.

I detected a great deal of fear in the area of the palm where Paul's birth was recorded. Even his aura was clouded with fear. Hesitantly, he inspected a sky blue chair before sitting on it. Paul was in his mid 30's, tall and gaunt with a worried look about him. Anxiety and panic attacks occurred with alarming frequency throughout his life, and he couldn't understand why. His doctor had prescribed medication to manage his symptoms, but every time he tried to discontinue the pills, the panic returned.

While tuning into this very important area of Paul's palm, I saw pictures of his mother – a very frightened young woman, unmarried and ashamed of her condition. Finding herself pregnant and alone, some 30 or more years ago, would have presented a totally unacceptable situation in their country of origin. To further complicate matters, the political climate had been quite unstable – not the best time to be bringing a child into the world, especially alone. The unfortunate consequence of this situation was that Paul ended up spending his whole life battling fear. Fear of failure, fear of success, fear of life itself.

The circumstances surrounding Paul's birth lay buried deep inside his subconscious mind. Upon gently uncovering and drawing out this Karmic fear pattern, Paul was finally able to understand why he was forced to deal with fear issues all his life. It was necessary for him to "open that forbidden doorway to the past", to identify the problem, so that he could begin to face his fears instead of allowing them to engulf and paralyze him.

He started reading books on how to handle fear and joined a "panic support group". The last time I spoke with him, he still had a lot of personal work to do; but he sounded much happier and more confident about himself and his life path.

It was important that Paul figure out the origin of his fear, to get right down to the root of it all, before he could begin to heal. For him, this meant going all the way back to the time of his birth. Then and only then, could he begin making progress towards healing the fear issues that were threatening to take over his existence. The decision to do something about his life, to take action and make the positive changes he needed was his, not mine. The ball was in his court and he chose to hit it!

Exhuming the past can be a traumatizing experience. Why not just leave it alone? Well, sometimes it *is* best just to leave it alone, but other times it is necessary to confront old issues. Blocking out the pain of a traumatic experience to minimize the hurt is a survival technique. But after a while it may pop up in your dreams or lodge itself in your body, like an annoying splinter in your finger. To continue blocking the pain puts us in a state of denial. We think we are getting over the problem (i.e. broken relationship, job loss, etc.) but in reality by not dealing with the issues that caused the pain in the first place, we are actually compounding the problem.

When an emotion like anger or resentment is suppressed long enough, it remains in our physical body and eventually manifests as an illness. Think of a fracture, or a broken bone that has not healed properly and bothers you with an annoying, dull ache. The sharp, excruciating part is over, but it still doesn't feel right, and every once in a while, surfaces to remind you that this "unfinished business" is still here.

So, you have a choice:

1) to continue ignoring the pain.
2) to acknowledge the hurt (yes that means facing it again) for the purpose of neutralizing or releasing the issue.

If you choose 1) it will never heal properly and will always bother you. If you choose 2) the bone will have to be re-broken (yes, that means going through the pain once again), reset properly and then the healing process can begin. Once properly healed, you can finally **let it go**.

Easier said that done. Who wants to repeat the pain and trauma of the past? Who wants to dig in deep and re-break that already painful bone that did not heal properly in the first place? Who wants to repeat experiences best forgotten?

Kim came to my booth at an Alternative Health Fair. Fortunately, she arrived at a time when there was a lull in the activity. It was suppertime, and most people had gone out to get something to eat. Calm, blue eyes looked out at me from an unruffled, pretty face. Deep rose lipstick enhanced a lovely smile. Her face told me one story, her hands quite another. Kim wanted to know if she would ever be happy and at peace. Uncomfortable feelings haunted her waking hours, as well as her dreams. She felt uneasy, like something or someone was watching her. Fear and anxiety overwhelmed her several times a week for no apparent reason. To make a long story short, she was unhappy with herself.

On the outside looking in, she was living an ideal life. She had a loving husband, two adorable children, and evidently no financial worries. What was causing these restless, painful feelings deep inside her? Why couldn't she let go of them?

After looking at her palm and feeling into her pain, the first words out of my mouth were, "You certainly had a rough time as a child." This intentionally generalized statement was enough to open up the floodgates. All of her stored-up pain came pouring out. Hers was a sad history of childhood abuse. Kim's family advised her years ago to "forget it – leave the past alone." Ordinarily, or with someone else, that might have been good advice, but not for Kim.

Subsequently, the whole reading focused on her past; her abusive childhood. Kim was unprepared for the reading to have taken this turn. Needing reassurance, she had come to me so we could peek ahead into her future. When would those uneasy, unhappy feelings leave her? What she did learn from the reading, was that the past had to be dealt with first – the real source of her unhappiness.

Fortunately, we were able to spend a little more time together than usual. There was nobody else waiting for me. People were still not back from supper yet, leaving most of the surrounding booths empty and allowing us a little more privacy.

Drying her eyes and composing herself once again, Kim looked straight at me and said, "You know, everyone told me to forget the past, but you were the first person to allow me to acknowledge it. I couldn't bury it without first validating it. Yes, this really did happen to me. Yes, I have permission to get angry about it. Now that I have faced it, I can finally begin to put it to rest.

"Before today, I felt like I was forced to deny it all. It was as though it had never really happened to me, when all along I knew that it had. I was constantly battling with myself. You helped me to bring it out in the open, face it, and now I can go on with my life."

Needless to say, Kim had come to a turning point in her life. Opening that forbidden doorway to look back through the years took a tremendous amount of courage. Now she could finally begin her journey toward inner healing. As she walked away smiling, I noticed a lightness to her step that wasn't there when she first walked into my booth.

Opening doorways to the past can be like opening Pandora's Box. What will you find? How will you deal with the darkness? Challenges? Consequences?

The most difficult part of your healing journey is having to confront your pain, hurt, and betrayal. How can you change your feelings? How do you release painful emotions? How do you just get over it?

I once wrote a column for the "The Journal of Alternative Therapies", a Montreal, Canada based publication. Readers were encouraged to write letters expressing their questions and concerns. One such letter was from Bob. He explained in his letter that he had hit rock bottom with nowhere to turn. What could he do? Every area of his life was in shreds.

I wrote back:

Sometimes the only way we will make a change in our lives is when we are forced to. Our situations become so intolerable that we simply have to find a way out.

Look back over your life and think about other times when you felt sad, lonely or let down due to a job loss, relationship break-up, or whatever. You did not get what you wanted or expected out of life and so you felt depressed. Now in retrospect, didn't that "bad luck" turn out to be for the best after all? Did another more suitable job or career come your way? Did another person come into your life – someone with her own rare qualities and special love to share with you? Or did you choose to feel sorry for yourself, blaming others for your misfortune? It sounds, from your letter, like you are searching outside of yourself for the solution to your problems. Who better to help you than you, yourself?

If you invariably look outside yourself for answers, you will never develop your own strengths, but will constantly take on everyone else's solutions, opinions, strengths and weaknesses. The only way out of your trap is to focus on making yourself the very best person you can be – for you. No one will magically appear to save you. You are your own savior. Once you get to know the "inner you" and gain deeper insight into your talents and strengths, you have a foundation upon which to rebuild your life.

Losing everything we have or had is a stripping away of the old in preparation for the new. You can't grow if you are stuck in the past (past relationships, past experiences, old ideas, old methods of carrying out business). If you have lost all your possessions, your wealth, even your loved ones, they have gone out of your life for a reason. They are no longer "right" for you and your personal growth at this point in time.

I am not trying to minimize how excruciating the pain can be, nor the feelings of helplessness you experience when the rug has been pulled out from under you. Some people spiral downwards in these situations to the point of severe depression and hopelessness. Sometimes you have to go there for a while until you get to a point where you say "no more!", then slowly begin your ascent back to the normal world.

Instead of focusing on the nightmare and asking "Why me?" focus instead on preparing for a new future. Open yourself up for the wonderful, new, good and exciting experiences and people who now have room to come into your life. The worst thing you (or anybody) can do when you are down at the bottom of that dark hole, is to concentrate all your energy on feeling rotten, helpless or encouraging more pain by feeling powerless.

You are being presented with a situation, or set of circumstances and it is up to you how you handle it. Right now you appear to be in the painful stage. It's OK. Just remember that it won't last, unless you make it last. Once you decide to say good-bye to sadness and go on to the next stage, you will be beginning your upward climb towards the light.

Look for the joy, the opportunities, the silver lining as the old saying goes. Turn your negative patterns into positive ones and you will see how quickly you regain your balance. Change your insides (thoughts, attitudes, perception) and your outside circumstances will change too – so will your lines!

Changing emotions or feelings that... hurt!

Now that we've "dug up the past" and confronted our pain, how do we let go of it?

Whether stuck uncomfortable emotions originate in the past or not, we need to deal with them now – today. How do you do that? How can poor Bob change from feeling destitute into feeling happy? Sounds tough.

One way to change emotions is to find the polarity or flip side of the anger, hurt, frustration. Pleasure, joy, fulfillment, happiness sound good, don't they? Let's see how this works. Your lover left you for someone else. How painful is that? Excruciating, ripping, tearing, empty, betrayed. It hurts! Feel your pain. Don't deny it. Feeling is part of life. If you don't feel, then you're not alive! Set yourself a deadline for grieving. Grieving is a natural part of the process. Remember Luba from Chapter 1? She grieved for her husband for years, until one day she resolved to go on and enjoy the rest of her life.

Turn the pain into pleasure, by seeking out and concentrating on the good aspects of this situation. This step can be rather tricky. First of all, you need to be ready. Next, if you can place a little distance between yourself and this betrayal or heartache, it will be easier. In other words, detach and try to look at this painful experience objectively, as if it happened to somebody else. Feel thankful that your ex-lover is no longer with you since he or she wanted out anyway. Take pleasure in remembering the good times, the learning experiences you shared…And know that you will share similar or more exciting and profound experiences with someone else.

The challenge lies in finding the opposite emotion, focusing on the happier, good feeling emotion, until you feel a change away from your present uncomfortable situation to a more relaxed or accepting state of mind (and body).

Get your body involved. Once you learn to catch your negative thoughts (blaming, guilt, pain), take notice of how your body feels just then. . Are you tense, muscles tight, as if waiting for the ax to fall? What's happening to your breathing? Stop right there and change the way your body feels.

Start by breathing deeply. Let go a little. As you allow your body to open with each breath, you will feel a change in your posture. Think of something you love to do and notice how your body responds. Imagine basking in the sun, floating through the clouds in a hot air balloon, walking barefoot through the grass morning dew between your toes, curling up all nice and cozy before a warm, crackling fire while snow swirls gently outside your window. Do you feel your muscles relaxing, tension easing? How is your energy level? Are you starting to feel a pull; a desire to plunge back into the stream of life once more? Practice switching from a negative, constrictive body posture to a positive, happy, relaxed state of being, and you will have learned a valuable technique.

Are you getting the hang of it? Let's look at another situation. Suppose you have to move. Your landlord kicked you out, or someone in your household gets transferred to another location. You don't want this; didn't ask for it (or maybe you did on another level). You are hurt and angry at this unexpected change just now.

We'll turn this around. What's the opposite of anger? Joy. You need to look for the joy in this situation. The old house or location no longer suits you, so you have to move on. This could be a wonderful opportunity for a fresh start. Your move to a new community is almost certain to bring you new friends, new experiences and a whole new outlook on life.

Life is so full of opportunities that there is always something better waiting around the corner. All you have to do is visualize this new goal and bring it towards you. Make it happen. And just how do I do that, you might ask? By your attitude.

Once you stop dwelling on the pain, despair, frustration, betrayal, etc. and focus on the challenge, joy, creativity of a new situation, then you are inviting good things into your energy field. Let go of the old and open up to allow and magnetize the new. Remember to keep your body involved by practicing your new technique. With a relaxed, happy body, you are open and living in the moment, in the now, not blocking out good energy with tense, unhappy muscles.

The other magic ingredient for success on how to turn negative attitudes into positive ones, is – faith or trust in the process. You've heard of the expression "When the student is ready the teacher will appear?" Trust the process. Everything will come to you at the right time.

As we move into acceptance of our situation, we understand that whatever happens is meant to happen. There is a Buddhist saying "Everything is as it should be". This doesn't eliminate our suffering, but helps us to accept our fate, so we can learn to deal with it. This "painful stage" can be as temporary as you want it to be. You don't have to be in pain forever. You have the power to make this stage as short or as long as you wish. Do you enjoy suffering? Do you enjoy playing victim? Well then, this will be a long stage (some people spend the rest of their lives in sorrow).

Let's expand on this picture by looking at one of the most primitive, painful of the negative emotions: **abandonment** Feeling unloved. Feeling alone. Devastated. Total blackness.

Have we all been abandoned at some point in our lives? Why

do we experience this incredibly strong fear literally ripping out our guts, leaving behind open wounds; wounds that partly heal, only to be torn open time and time again? What an acutely traumatic experience to be left totally alone and cut off from the rest of the world. It's frightening to feel so alone. It's devastating to feel the pain of abandonment, when someone we love and care for deeply, cruelly walks away from us, or dies and leaves us behind.

When it's someone who we've always looked up to for our care and nurturing, our emotional well-being, someone we thought loved us unconditionally, we suffer immensely.

Let's zoom in on the core issue here. What is the strongest force in the universe? Love, of course. Love is creation. Love is the beginning. Love is the root, strong enough to give life, and to nurture and support the very foundations of our being and of life itself. A loss of love hurts; leaves an emptiness inside, and consequently these very foundations are vigorously shaken up. How do we deal with this? Do we allow this loss to erode, crack and destroy our foundations?

Or do we accept and allow the earthquake, the shaking up of our world, knowing in our hearts that we will not be swallowed up or destroyed; that we will still be here when it is all over. Will we suffer? Yes, without question, but we will survive, if we so choose.

Now it's time to move on to getting rid of the paralyzing fear brought on by abandonment. We'll start by facing that fear – not shrinking from it. Face your fears and you have begun the process of dissipating the power of this huge monster.

Just the act of mustering up your courage is powerful enough to create subtle changes in your energy field. These subtle changes allow for your feelings to shift from a loss of control to a position of being in control or in the driver's seat.

Having the courage to face our worst fears puts us in a position of strength, so we can effectively deal with the situation at hand. Burying our head in the sand in denial, or pretending we're not hurt gets us nowhere.

Even if it's an unbearable pain, we still need to find the time and patience to handle it, otherwise, the pain will persist. What we resist - persists. In other words, by not dealing with our pain, we compound the problem – like the broken bone example earlier on in this chapter, or like a rotten apple in the apple barrel. If you take it out and throw it away immediately, you have looked after the problem and can go on to enjoy the rest of the apples.

If you leave the rotten apple in the barrel, not only will you still have a rotten apple, but it will spread to the other apples as well, and do far more damage. Eventually, you will have to deal with the problem and throw out more apples (or repair more damage) than if you had looked after the problem in the first place.

Abandonment – an instinctive primordial fear. Being left naked and exposed to die alone. No one to reach out to. No one to care. What does it mean in today's times? Are we so dependent on others for our emotional nourishment, for our love?

Most of us would heartily agree. If that is so, we risk living our lives as puppets, always being at the beck and call of others' feelings and opinions of ourselves. Think about it – we are allowing other people to tell us how to feel. In other words, we are determining how we feel based on another's judgment of who we are. If they feel loving towards us, we feel on top of the world, but conversely, if they are angry or self-absorbed, we feel depressed. Does it make sense to be at the mercy of other peoples' feelings? What about our own opinion of ourselves?

Do we care so little about what we think and feel about ourselves, about our individualities? Each one of us is unique with our own life force, our own special light, glowing deeply inside. Do we choose to nurture that light within, allowing it to glow with pride, respect and love for ourselves, or do we allow outside forces and negative emotions to extinguish and/or transmute our shining light?

"But," you may protest. "I am not an island. I need other people in my life." Yes, of course we do. We were not meant to live alone, cut off from others. We raise families and teach our children to love others as well as themselves. We give love and receive love. We care about other people. However, there is a significant difference, a fine line to cross in looking to a mate, partner, parent, or child to fulfill *all* of our needs.

In a loving relationship, we do count on our partners for understanding and support. But time and time again, we get caught up in unrealistically expecting a partner to "always be there for us". Stop and think: would they be happy neglecting their own needs in order to look after ours? Imagine how much more confident we would feel, if we could just remember our own special inner light, know we are worthy of our own love, and not constantly worry about how others feel towards us.

At the Palmistry Centre in Montreal, Canada, I was taught this saying "I love you and it's none of your business". This translates to: "I love you unconditionally with no expectations. I feel good knowing that I love you and it is reflected in my aura. I glow. Since like attracts like, in this loving state, I will attract positive people and life experiences to me. Whether you choose to return my love or not, is your business." Idealistic? Certainly. Are there really people out there evolved enough to embrace this philosophy? Of course.

It's helpful to say to yourself, "What is the worst that can happen? I will be left alone." Not a very comforting thought, is it? What is comforting is choosing to be enlightened enough to realize that we are not totally helpless, that we do have a measure of control over our actions and reactions to distressing situations that we absolutely cannot change.

I was teaching a course in Creative Visualization. Our Healing Circle consisted of a group of about 10 ladies. The goal of this course was to teach students to think positively and recognize their dreams, with the intention of creating a happy, healthy, prosperous lifestyle. (Creativity is the function of the right brain.)

In an atmosphere of this kind (soothing meditation music, candles, casual sitting on the floor and the personal nature of our discussions), emotional issues are often triggered. (This is the right brain coaxing the body to participate.) It was my job to provide a supportive, "safe space" to allow these feelings to surface, offering the opportunity for healing, not only for the student, but for the group as a whole.

Synchronicity draws specific people together. Contrary to outward appearances, this doesn't happen randomly. These people share common experiences, karma, and find parts of themselves reflected in other members of the group.

This cold Sunday afternoon was to be our second class, the first having been held the previous Sunday. I parked the car as usual in the parking lot and walked across the street and up to the front door. The front door was an outside door leading to several inner studios or rooms. I tried turning the knob, but nothing happened. It was locked. Strange. Again and again I turned and twisted that cold, unrelenting hunk of metal (knowing all the while I was wasting my energy). I even thought of kicking the door, but decided that I would only hurt my toes.

My classes were held in the studio of a friend of mine, Lena, who practiced aromatherapy massage. She had a lovely, fresh-looking healing space, alive with green plants and skylights; fragrant scents of lavender, jasmine, citrus, or spring flowers lingered delicately in the air.

This week, however, Lena was away on holiday, but she had assured me that the common front door would be open. If not, I was to go to the health food store next door and they would open for me, since they owned the building. Guess what? The health food store was closed. Now what? I muttered to myself. Since it was February and a windy, cold day, I walked back to my car to wait inside. After a while my ladies started arriving.

"We're locked out," I announced. Deciding to wait and see if anyone appeared at the health food store, we stood around the parking lot, stamping our feet and jiggling our bodies to keep warm. Since the parking lot was right across the street, we had a clear view of the whole building. In the space of a few minutes, every one of my faithful students arrived except for one – Joyce.

"Why don't we go to my house and have the class there?" suggested Lynn. Everyone agreed, so we piled into our cars and followed Lynn home. I had an uncomfortable feeling that Joyce was going to show up the minute we left.

'Perhaps you should stay and wait for her,' a soft little voice whispered inside my head (sounding suspiciously like Jiminey Cricket).

'No, no, we're already running late; if she were coming, she'd be here by now,' answered an impatient, louder voice.

Giving in to voice number two, I followed the ladies to Lynn's home.

That evening Joyce called me at home before I had the chance to call her. Was she ever angry! "How could you have the class without me?" She shouted into my ear. "I don't think I want to come back to any more of your classes."

"Well, we waited for you, but you didn't come." It sounded lame, even to my ears.

'See!' chided Jiminey Cricket.

Apparently Joyce's husband had dropped her off at the front door, waved goodbye and left. She had no money to call anyone and was not dressed for the bitter cold. Finding the doors locked and no one in sight, she felt totally and utterly abandoned. How we missed each other remains a mystery. Joyce is a 52-year-old woman, not a child; but throughout her life, she has had to deal with abandonment issues. As a little girl, her mother often left her to be cared for by strangers. She married at the tender age of 19 and not quite a year into her marriage, her husband committed suicide, leaving her alone with an infant. Why was this issue resurfacing now at this time in her life?

I calmed her down and threw out the suggestion that we hold a make-up class for her and Lena, since Lena had been away and missed this one too. "Oh, that's a wonderful idea!" she exclaimed, clearly happy once more. "How about tomorrow night after work?"

Synchronicity must have been playing a role here, because this whole episode was "meant to be". The following night during that make-up class, Joyce felt safe enough to open up and share her story. We were a small group (just 3 of us) so what Joyce couldn't express in front of the whole group, she could with our smaller, intimate one. As we listened to her and shared her pain, a bond began to form, drawing the three of us closer together. Through tears and hugs, I intuited a deeper understanding of this frightened soul. Outside our little circle, the energy in the rest of the room was strangely silent,…waiting. Time had no meaning. I had a strange feeling of being transported back to ancient times; it felt like we were reliving an experience that had taken place eons ago. I knew instinctively that we were deeply involved in a crucial healing process.

Joyce was only now facing her abandonment issues and had much internal processing to do. Somewhere in a deep, dark part of her soul, she must have felt it essential to hold on to her pain, for the length of time that she did; as if by letting it go, a part of her would vanish as well. By the time we were through, her aura was perceptively lighter. The gray cloudy areas that had clogged her energy field were dissipating, leaving her looking softer and more relaxed. I felt intuitively that this was just the beginning. The roots of her pain had grown exceedingly deep over time and I realized she had a lot of work ahead of her. Fortunately, she decided to continue with the classes, and in the process, learned to overcome some of her emotional blocks.

How do we rid ourselves of this ageless, timeless fear? How

can we release these unhealthy emotions so we can go on with our lives?

This difficult process takes time and consists of several steps. The first and most vital step is simply to feel your feelings. Feel the hurt or anger or fear. Feel the pain. These are your feelings – validate them. You have a right to feel what you feel. It need not be logical. Most of the time feelings are not logical. They're not supposed to be logical – that's the job of the left side of your brain. The feeling part belongs to the heart.

Can you relate to this? I am waiting for my husband to come home from work. It is now 7:00 and he told me he would be home by 6:30. He is only half an hour late, but already it feels like half a day. And he's never late! Supper is ready. Where is he? Another half hour drags by. Now I'm really getting worried. I wonder what's wrong. Maybe he's had an accident! Oh no, why didn't I give him a kiss this morning, instead of just waving at him.

My body grows tense, nervous, waiting for the phone or the doorbell to ring. I visualize him lying in a hospital bed, all smashed up, or worse. (This scenario is the work of the right side of the brain – it just loves to dramatize and drag the body into its fantasy.) I restlessly pace the floor, glance at the clock, and out the window. I look at the phone. Ring, I command. It remains quiet. I look at the door. Door – open, I command. And it does. "Hi!" he calls, in a cheerful, loving voice. "Sorry I'm a little late."

Like the air hissing out of a balloon, I deflate and my silly fantasy goes up in smoke.

So, logical or not, you feel the feelings, no matter how dreadful they are. Next, express them. You can write them down on paper. Writing them down not only clarifies what you are feeling and why, but allows you a certain amount of detachment. Problems are always easier to handle when they belong to somebody else. Get rid of them. Get them out of your mind and onto the paper. Then, burn the paper or cut it up in tiny pieces and throw it away or flush it down the toilet.

Make a ritual of it.

This simple symbolic gesture will help tremendously in cleansing yourself of troublesome, pessimistic feelings and emotions.

On a more physical level, you can yell and scream, jump up and down, or go down the basement and spend hours punching a punching bag. Some people run miles, or take long, brisk walks to let off steam.

Toning or humming is also a good way to express and release negative feelings and vibes. It is a method of releasing through your voice; a therapy that has its roots in ancient times (think of tribes of people, drumming and chanting to chase away evil spirits).

Light a candle or incense and just sit quietly with yourself for a while. When you are ready, ask yourself: "Is there a sound that wants to come out?" Listen for a moment and then express whatever sound comes to you. It could be an oooooooh, or an ahhhhhhh, a hisssssssss, or a cackle or a vavavavoom! It can be a loud blast or a gentle humming. Just let it all out, without getting your mind involved. Don't think self consciously how silly you must sound; nobody is around to hear you anyway - just allow the feelings and emotions. Give them space to be, without judgment.

Continue toning or voicing that particular sound until it changes. Then, using your intuition, go wherever your voice takes you; in other words, change the sounds when you feel moved to or continue the same tone over and over until you feel ready to stop. Give your voice free reign and don't be afraid of the feelings that come to the surface.

When you've finished, give yourself a few minutes to rest. Blow out the candle and ground your energy if you need to. Sit on the ground and just feel yourself in the arms of Mother Earth, supporting and comforting you.

Now it's time to move on to the next and final stage of this process. Your brain is tired of thinking, analyzing and rationalizing. Your fingers are tired of writing. Your voice is tired of toning and you've done as much jumping, punching and running as you can. In short, you've exhausted every avenue of expression you can think of. You've put out and expressed all that energy, but there is one more thing to do.

Bodywork. Go for a massage or a reflexology session. Take a shiatsu, acupressure or Reiki treatment. It doesn't matter what you try, in the sense that one is better than another, just choose whatever you are drawn to. As you are receiving your massage or body treatment, images or memories will come into your awareness that need to be released *from your body* – not your mind. Your mind has done enough talking and analyzing. Let it go and allow your thoughts to drift. Old scenarios may weave through your consciousness; events you haven't thought about in years. You haven't chosen to conjure them up – the act of massaging your muscles has given free rein to your emotions allowing them to come forth.

I remember lying on the massage table for the first time, relaxing deliciously under the fingers of the trained masseuse when out of the blue flashed an old painful memory. I had just been fired from my first job and was crying my heart out! (I was 18 years old at the time.) My employer had called me at home during my sick leave, to inform me that my "services were no longer required". Just like that. Poof! My job was gone – and so was my self-esteem. Holding back tears, I ran up to my bedroom to cry alone, not wanting my family to see how much it hurt. After a while, I shrugged off the pain; covered it up behind a forced smile, hoping it would go away. Obviously it didn't. This humiliating episode had happened more than 20 years before that day on the massage table! I was appalled! I didn't have a clue about cell memory in those days, but evidently had buried that "hurt" way down deep.

Over the years I learned that repressed emotions can get "stuck" in your muscles causing tension and pain. Every memory you have is stored in your body at the cellular level. Releasing these emotions trapped in your cells' memory can only be done through working directly on the tissues of the body themselves.

Once the mental work is done, having someone work on your body is like putting the roof on your house, butter on your popcorn, or whipped cream on your frappuccino. The finishing touch. Or you could think of it as simply a holistic approach. Work on both the mind *and* body.

So we don't get confused, this kind of body work is different than the "slamming the door to express anger" kind of body involvement. If you are having a reflexology treatment, there is nothing for you to do. You receive the treatment. The energy comes towards you. You don't push the energy away, like you would punching the pillow.

The healing happens as you unconsciously or unintentionally liberate trapped emotions. Again – there is nothing for you to do or *consciously* work through. Let your mind rest and be open to receive whatever it needs.

What about the spiritual? Isn't that a component of a holistic approach? Of course, and as far as the spiritual is concerned, I believe that that's where faith comes in. Believe that you are being guided to do what is right for you. Believe in yourself. Without that belief in yourself, you've already shut the door on Faith and swept Hope down the front steps and out with it.

All right – now you've done all that work – then what? It's time to fill the empty spaces with healing light and love. (Remember you've let go of horrible memories and feelings and left holes behind.) Focus on yourself for a while. Concentrate on truly loving yourself as you are, with all of your strengths and weaknesses, for this will create your foundation – your formula for living a successful, fulfilling, happy life. If this concept sounds strange to you – bingo - you've just found the root of your problem. Loving yourself should not be a foreign concept, but a natural state of being.

Strengthening ourselves through self-love is the first building block in the process of our own mastery. Encourage and support yourself by doing things you love. Take some time off work and enjoy a sunny afternoon, eat a gooey chocolate sundae, learn Japanese cooking, go on a holiday, play the drums, make a quilt. Enjoy life. If you've performed badly or made a mistake, don't beat yourself up. Give yourself the love and support you'd give your best friend. Tell yourself it's o.k. to make mistakes. People who don't make mistakes are people who never do anything!

Once we feel comfortable about loving ourselves, we can move on to enjoy intimate relationships with others, without the pitfall of being totally dependent on the other person. Remember, the world is constantly changing, and with it our experiences and feelings, day by day, month by month, year by year in our cycle of life. Nothing remains the same forever.

We will never eradicate totally the fear of being left alone, but what we can do is learn how to handle each situation as it comes up for us. Life is what we make of it. If we accept that people leave our lives because they no longer fit (we are changing and evolving at different rates), the hurt will be easier to deal with and further internal growth will take place. Accepting what we can't change, in addition to gaining wisdom from each experience (instead of focusing on sorrow and self-pity) are wonderful tools to help us "smoothly sail through" these negative experiences as we grow and stretch towards the light.

Speaking of our bodies, cell memory, etc., whatever we are going through on an emotional level ends up manifesting in our physical bodies to get our attention. In this way (through the physical body) we are alerted to the deeper issues struggling to make themselves known. This is nature's way of saying: "Hello! There's a problem here that needs your attention!"

Junella came to me about a year ago. She was a friendly,

attractive woman with a cheerful smile. Her aura was a soft cloud-like pink, interlaced with spongy areas of charcoal gray – her troubled areas. Junella's reading was progressing nicely when suddenly I sensed that there was something very much troubling her.

"What is it?" I asked her outright, letting go of her hand and shifting my focus to her face. Her powder-blue eyes reflected a deep sadness, as her cheery mask fell away. Tears filled those lovely eyes, and the real reason for her visit emerged.

"Will I ever be able to lose weight?" she asked in a quivery little girl voice. Surprise must have shown in my face, for she suddenly looked away. Quickly recovering, I mentally reassessed her outward appearance. That she was heavy was obvious, but to ask my advice on something, which only she had the power to control, caught me off guard. In a twinkling, I realized that this woman must be at the end of her rope.

A rush of information was suddenly transmitted to me through my intuition frequency:

Junella had dieted on and off for most of her life, with no lasting results. Nothing worked. Each new diet followed the same old pattern. She would religiously follow the rules; count her calories carefully and avoid all the things she loved to eat – chocolate, sweets, french fries and pina coladas.

At first her weight quickly and easily melted away. Thus encouraged, she'd start to feel good about herself. She was "doing" something constructive, not passively "wishing" to be slimmer. "I'm going to lose so much weight and be so skinny that I'll WOW everybody in a bikini!" she bubbled over to her fluffy white cat. Snowflake, of course, was not amused.

Turning away from her pet, Junella went to work leafing through magazines, looking for pictures of models wearing sexy bathing suits. Once found and clipped out, they would be taped to the refrigerator as an incentive to stick to her diet.

"Oh no, not another diet!" teased Tara, her slender 13-year-old daughter, after spotting her Mom's pictures of bikini-clad models on the fridge. "I'm going to eat at MacDonald's!" With a theatrical sigh, she turned to the cat. "Wadda you say Snowflake?" Snowflake responded by washing her face.

Thanks a lot for your support, Junella thought, anger beginning to bubble up inside of her. It's hard enough to do this alone. I don't even have a husband to encourage me anymore. And you, my precious daughter, can pig out whenever you want and not gain an ounce. Not fair!

With tears rolling down her cheeks, she retreated upstairs to her room. As she closed her bedroom door, she could hear Tara tearing open a box of chocolate cookies, oblivious to her mother's hurt feelings. Feeling sad and lonely, Junella flopped down on her bed and lay there in the dark.

It seemed that all her good intentions were beginning to crumble. Discouraged, she stopped "depriving" herself and gave in to those persistent cravings: a chocolate bar mid-afternoon to give her energy a boost, a pina colada while making supper in the kitchen (while no one was looking) and then she'd be right back to square one. Whatever weight she had lost was put back on and then some! There was an empty space in her heart that she was constantly trying to fill with sugar and chocolate – two well-known love substitutes. Junella didn't understand that she kept slipping off her diet because the emotional cause for her excessive weight gain had not been addressed. After weeks of really trying, it was discouraging to have the old patterns return.

Tuning into her wavelength once more, I could sense the pain and frustration Junella had suffered for most of her life.

Gently picking up her hand once again, I started probing into her past. What had happened to her? Why did she feel she had to hide; to protect herself by putting on layers of fat? What was the emotional reason behind her gaining so much weight?

[3]Louise Hay in her book *Heal Your Body*, suggests that people who are overweight are afraid; are running away from feelings.

Often they are insecure, extremely sensitive and subconsciously reject themselves. By building layers of fat they are insulating or protecting their inner beings.

Other people protect themselves by building walls around their hearts and adopting an outwardly aggressive or "who cares?" type of attitude.

Digging up the emotional cause for excessive weight gain is essential if you want to solve the problem. Dieting alone won't do. It's a band-aid solution – like sticking a piece of tape over a broken window, hoping it will go away. It won't.

Of course proper nutrition through good eating habits is vital to promote and maintain a healthy body, but if you don't unearth the emotional cause, the old sugar or salt cravings will take over and crack the foundation you have so carefully taken the time to build - through your healthier lifestyle.

There are times when the cause is fairly easy to detect and understand. For example – losing a loved one through death or divorce is a traumatic experience. It hurts! Over-nurturing through eating too much in an attempt to stop the pain, is the way some of us handle this situation. As a result, the body produces layers of fat to protect hurt feelings.

Others do the opposite. They stop eating as an expression of their pain and under-nourish or reject themselves.

In other situations, the cause is more deeply rooted, going 'way back into childhood, with a resulting lifelong "battle of the bulge".

Looking at the beginning of Junella's Life Line, I could see that she had been separated from her mother shortly after her birth. Her mother had been very ill, requiring hospitalization when Junella was just a baby. Of course little Junella couldn't understand her circumstances back then, but did feel the separation from her Mom – her source of food – her lifeline.

As we discussed Junella's past, it became clear that separation issues surfaced over and over again throughout her life. In order to combat the accompanying feelings of rejection, Junella had turned to food for comfort and fulfillment. The larger she became, the more comfort she required, and 'round and 'round it went in a vicious circle.

Then one morning something snapped deep within Junella. Looking candidly at herself in the mirror, she realized at that moment that she did not even like herself. A part of her being quietly acknowledged that she had come to a crossroads; she had reached a turning point in her life; and had made a decision, on some deeper level, that it was time to change. Her old self did not fit anymore. It was time to do something to heal those wounds.

Junella's first step was to seek help. It was essential that she understand what had gone on in her past so she could let go of self-rejection and allow the door for compassion to open – compassion for that baby who experienced rejection at such an early age. Now she could begin to heal.

Where to start? I suggested she begin with affirmations, affirming love and acceptance of herself just the way she is.

I love and approve of myself just the way I am.

I am lovable.

It is safe to be me.

I create my own security.

I have a beautiful body, full of energy, vitality and joy.

The next step in the process was for her to adjust her perception of her body so that she "felt" like she was slim already. Living your dream, or as though you already have achieved your goals, will work at a subconscious level to bring what you desire closer to you.

"Why don't you come to my next Creative Visualization course?" I asked her. Creative Visualization is a wonderful way to make positive changes in your lifestyle – and yes – even your body!

Junella came back to see me recently. I was pleasantly surprised by her overall appearance. Her hard work had paid off rewarding her with a pleasing silhouette. She didn't need her layers of protection any more. Genuine happiness shone all through her aura. "Thank you," she said, "for starting me off on the right path." I looked at her and smiled warmly.

"So, now that that's done," she continued, her powder-blue eyes sparkling with new life. "How about telling me something fabulous – like when will I meet the man of my dreams?"

Laughing together, we began her reading. Junella had changed and so had her lines. When we were finished, she turned to me with a twinkle in her eye. "You never answered my question," she teased playfully. She was referring to her question at our first session. "Will I ever be able to lose weight?"

"I didn't have to." I replied with a smile. "The solution was there all the time – within yourself."

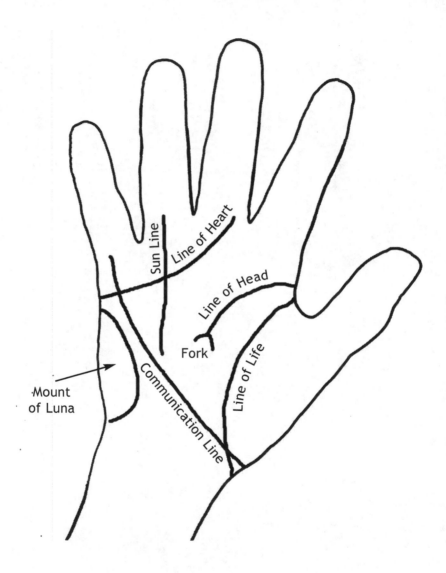

CHAPTER 5

IT'S ALL IN YOUR HEAD

Now we come to our Head Line – the third and last major line in our palms. The other two are – Life Line and Heart Line. If you remember, major lines express *subconscious* patterns of thought. The minor lines (and there are many more of them), express *conscious* patterns of thought.

If you want to make changes in your life, which do you think would be easier to change? Right – the conscious patterns of thought. The thoughts you are more aware of on a daily basis – the ones you have some control over. So it makes sense that when you are searching for line changes in your palms (as a barometer of what's happening in your life) it will most likely be the minor lines that are different; either evolving as they should, or giving you more problems to sort out. Changes in the major lines take much longer to develop and appear on your palm, because the issues run deep.

For example, your Sun Line (found snuggling up to your ring finger) is one of your minor lines. Your Sun Line is in charge of your attitude towards good fortune, money and having fun. If you believe you will live a life of abundance and good luck, then you will have a good strong Sun Line. Conversely, if you believe everyone is out to get you, you will have a short or even non-existent Sun Line.

Suppose you decide you've had enough of "bad luck" and want to change your attitude. Like anything else, it will take some resolve and work on your part, but if you have a clear intention and truly change your thoughts (lighten up and have more fun) and your attitudes (put down your burdens and take up belly dancing or salsa), then you will be rewarded with a long, strong Sun Line. It will be easier to change those thought patterns than it would trying to mend deeper issues, such as a broken heart.

Healing a broken heart (looks like a slash through your Heart Line), or drastically changing your lifestyle from one of apathy to vitality (reflected in the sweep of your Line of Life) is a far more difficult transformation to undertake, as these patterns originate in our subconscious mind, finding expression through the major lines in our hands.

So changing our patterns, our thoughts and attitudes is easier at the conscious level, and you can follow those changes by watching the minor lines in your palm evolve. Some of my clients do just that. They come back for a reading and want to know why their destiny line has changed, their line of travel has disappeared or what that new line means right over here? Understanding the reasons for these changes gives us a clearer picture of why readings done at different times will produce different results. How much *you* have changed will be reflected in the lines and markings in your palm. Doesn't it feel good to know that we have *some* measure of control over our lives?

Now, on to our Head Line. Our Head Line is a measure of our beliefs, our reasoning, and how we react to information; in other words, the nature of our thinking. It begins between the thumb and Jupiter finger and gently curves across the hand.

As with the Lines of Life and Heart, the intensity of your Head Line is important. The deeper the line, the more intense your thought processes will be. You think carefully before embarking on a project or entering into a friendship. You look at everything from all angles, and you don't have time for idle conversation or "fluff". Intense, deep Lines of Head belong to scientists and researchers.

Balance is important in evaluating the three major lines in your hand. If your Head Line is deeper than your Heart Line, then feelings will tend to be shunted towards your head for processing. "It hurts to feel, so you take over for a while," says your heart to your head. "Give me a break."

If you have a short straight Head Line, you are drawn to facts, mathematics and a down-to-earth approach to life. There is a certain amount of rigidity in your thinking. Things have to be done properly and there is not much room for deviation or interpretation. A successful banker, engineer, or farmer would belong in this category. Mind you, if you have creative markings in your palm (for example: a pronounced mount or a star under your ring finger) then you could very well turn out to be a *creative* finance person, engineer, or farmer – but let's not complicate matters, shall we?

A long sloping Head Line that flows into the middle of your palm, is called a "Psychologist's Head Line". People with this configuration are drawn to others, have a positive outlook on life and are always ready to listen to your problems with an empathetic ear. You can cry on their shoulders and they will put themselves out to help you. Subconsciously, they will choose healing professions, but not always. They are imaginative and inspiring, and prefer to make life interesting by weaving a bit of creativity into their daily routine.

An extremely long Head Line, going right across the palm and into the Mount of Luna, indicates someone with a profound imagination. These unique, fun-loving people are born with an imagination so strong that they often create and live in a world of their own. That is not so terrible. I'll bet the creators of Nintendo and other computer games and movies such as Star Wars have extremely long, imaginative Head Lines, as do artists, magicians, and students of the esoteric.

Some people have Head Lines reaching up towards their Heart Line, (as opposed to their Heart Lines dipping down to their Head Lines as seen in Chapter 3). The meaning is crystal clear: "Help! I'm tired of thinking, analyzing, and logic, how about *you* feeling your way through this muddle."

As noted before on the other lines in your palm, crosses, circles and breaks are signs of trouble. Head injuries, migraines, nervous breakdowns and depressions are all documented on your Head Line. Again, timing is important and can be read according to the location of the mark. Having advance warning or preparation may be enough to prevent you from potential pitfalls, illnesses or depression.

If your Head Line ends in a fork – you could be an unknown writer just waiting to be discovered! This "Writer's Fork" when combined with a strong Line of Communication is a good indication that what you write may very well be published. You could write screenplays, novels, textbooks, travel guides, poetry – the list is endless. Having a strong Communication Line will lead you to success in a career such as publishing, television, radio, theater, journalism, travel, teaching or computer skills of all kinds.

Diane came to see me with a decision to make. I was struck by the richness of her thick coppery hair as it cascaded down her back. Settling herself in a blue chair, she peered nervously at me through a pair of funky purple glasses.

"I really don't know what to do," she began. "I need to find a job, but nothing sounds right. My father wants me to work as a junior programmer in his computer company. I also have an opportunity to work as a sales rep for an audio-visual company. But, I really don't want to do either."

"Well", I began. "First of all, you chose to sit in a blue chair. Blue is the color of the throat chakra, which encourages us to: speak our truth and to express ourselves. You seem to be doing a good job so far. At least you can express what you don't want. Let's see what your hands look like."

Diane had long fingers with knotty joints. This suggested an analytical mind. (Hmmm, maybe she could be a lawyer, I thought). Her Head Line was separated from her Life Line at its origin telling me that she was a very independent person.

(Hmmm, a very good lawyer). As I examined her Head Line in depth, the possibility of a law career became even stronger. The shape and curve suggested not only intelligence, but also the ability to relate well to others, while maintaining a degree of detachment.

"How about studying law?" I inquired looking up at her. Diane nearly jumped out of her chair.

"Law!" she exclaimed. That was one of my teenage dreams, but I dug a hole and buried it deep. I'm not smart enough to be a lawyer."

"I think you may be in for a surprise, but let's do your numbers – just to make sure. What is your date of birth?"

"April 23, 1979."

"That adds up to an 8. Eight is the number of success, power and abundance. If you work your 8 vibration in the positive, your energy and hard work will be duly recognized. Also, you were born on the 23rd day of the month. Two plus 3 equals 5 – the number of communication. You will very definitely get your point across in a courtroom."

"So, what do you think?" I pushed (just a little).

"Oh my God." was all she would say.

Every once in a while I come across someone with a Head Line that has stopped and then starts up again some distance later; or a Head Line that seems to be in the wrong place. This is not something to look forward to. It means that this person will undergo a dramatic change in mental energy; shifting thought processes altering consciousness, sometimes to the point of a total breakdown.

It is vitally important to note which hand is involved. If this fragmented or strange Head Line is on the left hand (for a right-handed person), then the experience has thankfully, passed. When it appears on the right hand, I know that this person is in for a huge psychological adjustment; a redirection of their normal thinking pathways, which will dramatically alter their life path. This can be an overwhelming, distressing period to have to go through, so a sensitive, supportive approach is needed.

"I don't think so!" Sharon got up from her red chair and stomped out, her black ponytail flicking angrily from side to side. I had tried to be as gentle as I could, but I guess she wasn't buying it.

Sharon had a Head Line that was "off the wall". Her mercurial moods had gotten her in trouble many times over. Wanting to be herself, yet wanting to conform and be accepted by others was an ongoing battle within her soul. Mentally, she was stressed out. Forcing herself to conform to society's ways assured her acceptance as part of the crowd. Yet, she did not feel real. She felt like someone else, like a robot. The times when she openly rebelled, she felt people turning away, snickering, shunning her. And yet it was those very times when feelings of her own personal power, her authentic self, shone through. This internal "tug of war" was taking its toll on Sharon.

Dressed in a tight leather skirt and fishnet stockings, she paced the room before settling down. Her worn black leather jacket was flung carelessly on the chair next to her. A silver loop pierced her eyebrow and what looked like a miniature soccer ball grew out of her tongue. Purple streaks adorned her hair. I guessed she was in her early 40's - a long way from being a teenage rebel. Apparently, this was her "this is me, like it or not" phase.

"Here," she began by thrusting her hand under my nose. "Tell me something good." Her split head line jumped out at me, but, I waited.

"Everyone is against me, my family is against me."
I waited.

"I want to spend the rest of my life on the back of a motorcycle, cruising around. There's nothing wrong with that is there? Everyone says I'm irresponsible, but hey, I don't rob banks!"

"OK, let's start at the beginning." Her hand felt red hot, simmering with an unnatural energy and rage. I began by briefly dipping into her past. I thought it best to start slowly, recognizing her tolerance level to be low.

"Maybe," I ventured, "you might want to spend a bit of time by yourself to sort things out, before........"

That was all I could say before she stomped out of the room.

Not everyone with a split headline is as volatile as Sharon. Deep feelings often lie buried without a means of expression. Only the lines of the palm betray the inner person.

Rachel's separated Head Line arose from her feelings of betrayal. She had chosen to marry outside of her faith, and although very much in love, felt she was ultimately forsaking her birth family. To make matters worse, her father harshly chose to cut her off from being a member of their family, and her distress was obvious. The separation in her Head Line reflected her mental confusion; she could not grasp that her concept of life, as it had always been, was in the process of being completely, dramatically altered.

Gaby came back for another reading. Remember Gaby from Chapter 2? The lady whose life was lying all around her in shreds? I hardly recognized her. Her hair was cut in a layered fashion, accentuating her oval face and lovely cheekbones. She wore casual, but smart clothes with confidence. Her energy field was vibrant and happy and I suspected that she had a new love in her life.

Looking at her long curving Head Line, I had hoped she'd found a creative enterprise to tackle. The slope of her Head Line could also be interpreted as a "Psychologist's Head Line", but I knew that becoming a therapist would not work for her.

Gaby told me she'd tried to set up an internet business, but it didn't work out. She next applied for a job in a marketing company, but was not happy working in that environment for long. Then she decided that she might as well jump into life with two feet and try doing something she'd never done before.

She gave up worrying. She stopped thinking and planning and wondering what her next step should be. She stopped "doing" altogether. Instead she began observing, relaxing, and yielding to the flow of life.

One day while shopping for shoes, she accidentally overheard an employee of the store having a heated argument over the phone. She and her husband were fighting over whose turn it was to pick up their child from daycare, go home and start preparations for the evening meal. Apparently it was hubby's turn, but he had to put in overtime at his job, and this was causing chaos with their schedule.

After leaving the store, Gaby walked to her car while mulling over that conversation in her mind.

I wonder if there are more people out there in the same situation. I enjoy cooking. It relaxes me as I zone out everything but the ingredients that will eventually become a work of art or an arrangement. Instead of flowers or plants, I like using food – healthy food, of course. All those brightly colored fruits and veggies....... hmmm.......

And so, Catering from the Source was born. After some inquiries and networking, Gaby started cooking attractive, nourishing "home cooked" full course meals. Wholesome food for people on the run.

The "Source" part of it was baking everything from scratch – even the bread, pasta and sauces. This gave her a wide scope to create with dough or experiment with herbs and spices, thereby adding her own personal touch. In addition to looking scrumptious, everything tasted yummy with the added bonus of being home-cooked and nutritious. Her aim was to provide healthy meals for working people, and in that way she felt she was offering a valuable service. Using food as a building block, she was actually laying her own foundation, without really being aware of it. Back to basics meant starting over. She was not interested in international cuisine or catering weddings or conferences. There were plenty of people doing that.

Looking once more at the creative lines and signs in her palm, I knew that Gaby had the potential to expand her catering business over the next few years. Before I could say a word, however, she excitedly told me that she had further plans for the word "Source" in her company name; she wanted to go right to the source – all the way back to planting and harvesting the food she would use in her catering business. She could use her creativity to experiment with seedlings, cross pollination, and hydroponics.

To say I was pleased with Gaby's change of circumstances was an understatement. She was no longer afraid of trying new things, tackling a few challenges, while growing from within and sharing her gift of creativity. I wondered for a brief moment if she was biting off more than she could chew, but decided not to say anything. Her plans were certainly in the realm of possibility. It was me who had to adjust my thinking to this vibrant, new being. Right now, she was happy and I was pleased.

* * *

Readings are never wasted. There is always some good that comes out of it, even if it turns out to be a "bad reading". If you've chosen the wrong reader, it would be wise to come away with the lesson of trusting your instincts, or just being a little more discriminating next time. If the advice feels all wrong, disregard it, but bear in mind that there must have been a reason why you chose that particular reader. Maybe you just were not ready to accept what she was telling you, or it really was inaccurate. However, there is usually a grain of truth in something being spoken. Sometimes all you need is that one little spark, that one bit of information to boost you to higher ground, or stimulate your thought processes.

One evening, I went to a "channel party". The atmosphere was perfect. Candle glow provided the only light in this old and creaky, yet charming apartment. The guests sat around on chairs or cushions on the floor, drinking wine and nibbling tidbits. I couldn't help admiring the gleaming oak floors as I peeked under my cushion.

A subtle change in energy warned me that the "channeller" had arrived. I looked up to see her enter the room, confidently taking her place in the center of our circle. A respectful hush swept over our group.

"Everyone tonight will receive a message from the spirit world...." she began. We looked at one another in anticipation. Ohhh, what fun! What kind of messages would we get? Around the circle she went, delivering her messages to each person out loud so everyone could hear. When she got to me, I was disappointed, for the information she was giving me did not make sense at all. I put a false smile on my face and looked around. My trusty intuition was telling me that a lot of the other girls felt the same way. There were some, however, who seemed satisfied with their personal message. I came away wondering why I had ever gone to that party in the first place. It was a waste of an evening (even the wine was cheap).

For a long time afterward, I was unable to put this experience out of my head. I kept trying to analyze it, wondering what useful purpose it had served. After a while I did let it go, forgot about it. About two months later in a dream, I got the message to be extra alert when palm reading, to pick up and identify any problems with communication. To make myself clear. I was warned in my dream to remain open – not just assume that whatever I said was always correct.

Later on, I learned that this particular "channeller" had turned herself off to receiving negative feedback from her clients. In fact, she wasn't open to any feedback at all. I remember during that evening, if someone looked puzzled or said something like "I don't know what you are talking about," she would say. "The timing is wrong – that's all." And then move on to someone else.

As we travel along the road of life, it's nice to take a rest stop once in a while to consult our "map" before continuing on our way. And if we find a kindly soul, someone gentle and understanding, intuitive and wise to guide us on our journey, we have truly found the pot of gold that dwells at the end of the rainbow.

CHAPTER 6

GUARDIAN ANGELS, SOULMATES, AND PAST LIVES

Do you have a guardian angel? Would you like to find out if you do?

The best way to go about this is to schedule a bit of time when you can relax and be alone for a while. Choose a time when you won't be interrupted. Select a quiet room and make yourself comfortable. If playing soft music helps you to set the mood, by all means put on something soothing.

Once you are relaxed and in a quiet, receptive frame of mind, think back over your life's experiences. Let your mind be open, allowing the flow of memories to begin. Don't analyze anything, just focus on those memories.

Take your time and really look back over the years. If you are having trouble tuning in to your past, try to imagine yourself walking along a garden path. All along each side of the path see in your mind's eye scenes from your life going backwards in time.

Step off the path when a particular scene or memory pulls at you, or becomes more focused and brighter, wanting your attention. Follow that memory and let yourself re-live that experience. Don't rush the process; just let it happen.

For those of you who meditate, put yourself into a meditative state and ask for guidance.

One of those memories may take you back to a time when you were in trouble. Serious trouble! Or sick. Confined to bed and feeling like you were at death's doorway. Scared and vulnerable. Why is it when we're sick we feel so helpless, so awful? All at once something changed. In the space of a few minutes you went from weak and ill to feeling tingly all over, lighter or just

92

different. That heavy feeling in the air lifted, like clouds suddenly parting to reveal a clear blue sky. Relief washed over your entire being and somehow you *knew* that this illness would pass and you'd be well once again.

Do you remember feeling a presence in these times of trouble - a feeling as if someone or something was there with you? A subtle energy or change in the air, but you couldn't see anyone? Some people experience this presence as a voice or music, originating inside their own head. Others see a shimmer or flicker at the corner of their eye.

Does the memory of a loved one who has passed away suddenly pop into your head at odd times; or into your dreams?

If you answer yes to any of those questions, or feel that there is a presence guiding you, chances are, you have been in contact with your guardian angel.

If you look closely at your hand, you will see that your Guardian Angel Line closely follows the flow of your Life Line. These lines are always located *inside* your Life Line, towards your thumb, as if working quietly behind the scenes. Remember the "double trouble" lines 'way back in Chapter 1? These double Life Lines (for this is what they look like) can also, be called extra strength lines. They are helper lines in times of stress. When I point this out during a reading, I'm always met with a wry smile or a scornful laugh.

"Oh yeah. Right on. You're not kidding!" are some of the comments I usually hear.

People with these extra strength lines have them for a reason. Their lives are filled with many a rocky hill to climb and challenges to face. In spite of this, or because of this, they develop a resiliency, which enables them to recover from their predicaments fairly quickly. These are the people who pick themselves up, dust themselves off, and continue on their way. As well, these auxiliary lined folk posses a high standard of ethics, and won't tell a Soul if you choose to divulge all your secrets to them – really!

Back to Guardian Angel Lines – whether they are angel or extra strength lines, ultimately they are gold – pure gold, and are working to protect you. Some lucky people are blessed with not only one Guardian Angel Line, but several! Interestingly, this information takes them by surprise. Their eyes light up as they recount stories about one particular angel, but have not considered the possibility of more hovering about.

You may notice an Angel Line on your palm that looked strong and deep at one time, but is now fading away. This means that its time is up. This particular "being" or "guide" has accomplished what it was assigned to do and is now moving on.

By studying the length of these Angel Lines, and using good old intuition again, I can help you uncover the mystery of who your guardian angel really is. Tiny lines represent baby angels. Spirits whose bodies have crossed over in infancy. Baby angels or spirits are just as powerful as grown ones. Some of them connect to a small child and protect him or her for only a short period in their lives.

When I first started reading palms, I was amazed to learn that not only were some of my clients aware of having a guardian angel, but they also knew who their angel was! These clients just had a strong inner knowing that no matter where they were or what situation they were caught in the middle of, Grandpa, Great Aunt Betsy, Sister Rose or another presence was close by, watching over them.

Ha! And I thought I was being so smart, telling someone that they were being looked after by Grandmother Guardian Angel. They already knew! Fortunately, I've learned a lot since those early days of readings.

Some clairsentient people can feel a change in energy in the air when their angel is nearby. Clairaudient folks hear a shimmer of sound, like harp music or the tinkle of tiny silver bells, or even a wee little voice. People who perceive their world visually (clairvoyants) will catch a glimmer or sparkle in the air or actually see the form of an angel, before the spirit fades away.

For those of you who don't have a Guardian Angel Line on your palm – it doesn't mean you don't have a guardian angel. Your angel may just be a little shy or hiding for the time being. When the time is right, your angel will surface. Not *everything* is registered in your palm, nor does everyone register the same kinds of experiences in their palms. In other words, you can have one angel or several, without manifesting those lines in your hands.

I believe that *everyone* has a guardian angel. Yours may be a relative who has passed away, either recently or long before you were born. Or, someone from a past life, trying to re-establish a connection in this life. You share a special bond with this Soul Angel, who chooses to appear in your life now, helping you through the rough times. Perhaps you both have Karmic patterns to work through. Your guardian angel might also be a close friend who wants to remain in your energy field, or a spiritual being assigned to look after you. Whatever your belief system, angels have now chosen to spread their wings and publicly fly out into the open, making their presence known and felt.

Several years ago, a client of mine, Georgina, lost her young daughter to a fatal illness. Georgina knew and felt in her heart that she was still connected to her daughter, even though their roles were now reversed. The daughter was watching over her mother, rather than the other way around, as it had been when the little girl was alive.

Once upon a time, if you were to openly talk about guardian angels, people would have looked at you strangely and then likely crossed the road – pretending not to know you.

But not today! Angels are everywhere these days, and have been for quite some time. Walk into any novelty store and you will see pins, jewelry, greeting cards, artwork – you name it.

Popular now are enticing Angel Shops, where you can buy angel everything! I have angels peeking down at me from my kitchen walls, over the front door, and on either side of the fireplace mantle. Surprisingly, a few years ago, a wave of Angel sightings found its way into the newspapers and on national television. The surprising part was the reporting – not the sightings themselves.

What I find appealing about this angel "invasion" is the focus on feeling good. We, as a society, are moving in the direction of feeling good, on being loved and protected, rather than descending into a cold, unfeeling, mechanical society as predicted by George Orwell in his book 1984.

One cloudy afternoon, I was reading the palms of a group of hairdressers in a beauty salon. Vanessa, the proprietor, wanted to give her staff something different for Christmas, so she asked me if I would come in to the shop and read each hairdresser's palm. I agreed, so she closed her doors to the public just after lunch for the party.

My first client was Leslie, a pretty redhead. "Oh, you have a lovely Guardian Angel Line!" I told her, feeling the energy of a loving female Soul. Leslie looked surprised at first, but then her eyes narrowed suspiciously. "I don't think I believe in angels," she retorted with a shake of her head.

I was just getting ready to move on to something more interesting – like her love life or career path, when a strong feeling washed over me. It felt as if her guardian angel wanted me to say something. I waited a minute, allowing myself to become open, so I could channel the information.

"Your guardian angel has been trying to reach you, but you seem to be closed to her communication. Do you have any idea who she could be?"

"No." She frowned. Definitely time to move on here.

"Let's have a look at your Relationship Lines. I see you have two. One is rather weak and short, but the other one is clear and strong."

"Oh." That frown again.

"The first line," I continued, "(now we used to call those marriage lines, but today people don't always choose to marry, so I refer to them as Special Relationship Lines) is rather faint, indistinct, representing a past boyfriend or lover significant enough to leave....."

"Oh!" Leslie exclaimed, suddenly sitting up in her chair. "Margie. I've been thinking of Margie for the past while and I don't know why. In fact, the last time I thought about her, I nearly got myself killed, so I try to push her memory away when she pops into my head." She crossed her legs and sat back again.

"Who is Margie?" I asked gently.

"She was a good friend of mine, who died in a car accident about 3 years ago," Leslie recalled, blinking back tears.

The last time she had thought about Margie was around five or six months ago, while driving to work. She had a busy day ahead of her. Student hairdressers were scheduled to arrive in the salon, and although the extra help was welcomed, they disrupted the regular routine with questions and problems to be sorted out. Some of the clients enjoyed the young students, but others became impatient or asked outright not to have a student in attendance. Keeping up with the students' questions, while maintaining her customary high-quality service required the skill and balance of a tight-rope walker!

With these thoughts swirling around in her head, Leslie failed to see the familiar red "Stop" sign in front of her until it was too late. Car brakes screeched. Horns blared.

Snapping out of her reverie, she jammed on her own brakes just in time to avoid crashing into an oncoming car. As she sat behind the wheel shaking and frightened, Margie's face flashed across the screen of her conscious mind. She could feel strange currents in the air as if Margie sat beside her. Abruptly she turned to look at the seat next to her. It was empty. "Now I'm really going bananas," she mumbled to herself.

Strangely, Leslie didn't connect this experience with a guardian angel. Instead, she felt as if just thinking of Margie was bad luck.

As we unlocked yet another of Leslie's doorways to the past, we discovered that memories of Margie often popped into her head whenever she was in the middle of a crisis. At the end of her reading, I could see her aura beginning to change. A soft shade of violet subtly crept in to take over the darker areas of discomfort. With a calm, serene look on her face, she thanked me and made ready to leave. Leslie had no idea that I knew what she was thinking – underlying this peaceful persona, I could sense an undercurrent of excitement at the opening of a door to a new awareness – an awareness of being loved and protected by her own guardian angel.

Yes, guardian angels have chosen to wing their way into our lives and hearts these days, and the timing couldn't be better. The comfort and support they radiate is meant to help us through life's challenges in this fast-paced, unpredictable, but wonderful world we all live in.

How Do You Find Your Soulmate?

First of all, what is a Soulmate? A Soulmate is a deep and very powerful love relationship, someone who you connect with at every level of your being. Someone who cares about you. Someone who knows what you are thinking, what you are feeling – without words being exchanged.

You feel each other's feelings; as if you are sharing the same energy field. There are times when you feel pain or uneasiness in your own body for no apparent reason. You were fine this morning. What has changed? What is going on? Nothing terrible, just your Soulmate trying to communicate with you. He may be ill, or in a situation he would rather not be in.

Consciously or not, he is reaching out to you for help.

As you tune into your Soulmate's energy, it dawns on you that he or she is in trouble. Distance has no bearing on this kind of relationship. Oceans and mountains may separate you, but you always know how your Soulmate is feeling. There is no hiding of feelings in a Soulmate relationship. You are always on the same wavelength - a blending together of Souls.

A Soulmate feels like a part of you, like a twin (not to be confused with a Twin Soul). The two of you fit perfectly together like pieces of a jigsaw puzzle. Some people believe that a Soulmate relationship is a Karmic one, sharing many lifetimes over thousands of years. This is why recognition is instantaneous. You've been together before and when you find each other again, you know – you just know.

Twin Souls share a deep Soul connection. The relationship is intense, passionate and intimate. The attraction irresistible, addictive – you can't get enough of the other person. Even if it's someone of the same sex (and you're not that way inclined), you enjoy every minute together with a sharing that leaves other people out in the cold.

Magic happens when you're together – you want to be in each other's company exclusively. The feelings are *that* strong. Unfortunately, a Twin Soul usually comes into your life for a relatively brief period of time. This "catalyst" relationship serves as a stepping stone on your path. I say "unfortunately" because the parting is excruciatingly painful, like a tearing apart of your Soul. Neither of you understand how the other person, who you shared such a close and loving relationship with, can be taken away from you (and this is how you see it, no matter who leaves who). Through this relationship, a transformation takes place within, to prepare you for a higher learning experience. Or, if you are lucky, the arrival of your true Soulmate, a little further down your path. When that time comes, your true Soulmate will be in your life for always (many times over).

Melanie came to see me for a reading because she was concerned about her relationship. She confided to me that she had bonded with a girlfriend, and felt closer to Heidi than to her boyfriend. She was feeling guilty about this non-sexual closeness that she shared with another woman, thinking it strange that she could not share this same closeness with her boyfriend of many years. Melanie loved her boyfriend passionately, but once they had gone their separate ways to work each morning, the connection was broken. Of course she thought about Greg during the day, but it wasn't quite the same as sensing what was going on with him, or knowing when he was thinking about her.

The two women felt totally comfortable and at ease with one another right from the beginning. Melanie would get these funny feelings of "déjà vu" – feeling herself drawn back to the past, in another time, another life. The strange thing was, Heidi was there too! The girls never discussed these experiences – they didn't have to. Each person knew what the other was thinking, often instinctively feeling what the other was experiencing, no matter where they happened to be. Feeling closer to each other than to their own sisters, they often referred to themselves as "twins". So did other people.

"Oh, the *twins* just came in for coffee," called the servers to one another at the local coffee shop whenever Melanie and Heidi came strolling in. If one of the girls turned up alone, someone invariably asked where the other girl was. It was as if people sensed their Soul energy or bonding as twin Souls.

Skeptics may remark, "It sounds like they are just close friends. What's the difference?" The difference between close friends and twin Souls is:

1) The time frame: you can have a very close relationship with someone because you have known him or her for years. With Soulmates and twin Souls, this closeness is immediate... within the first few minutes or days of meeting that person.

2) The feeling and understanding aspect of the relationship. You always know how the other person is feeling. There is an uncanny, yet strong connection uniting the two people. This energetic connection surrounds the couple in a magic circle, which can be felt by some people, seen by others. The energy, which they sense instantly, bonds the two at every level, right to the very depths of their Souls. You totally understand your Twin Soul and they you, which results in an incredible sense of closeness. You share total loyalty, honesty and complete confidence in this relationship. Without question you accept each other's weaknesses and strengths. There is no room for envy or jealousy. All this is felt or sensed through a rare form of communication – no words are necessary.

With close friends you understand and accept each other, and can often predict behavior or reactions, but you don't always know how the other is feeling at a given time, especially when in different parts of the globe. That Soul connection is missing, so the strength of the tie that keeps you together loosens as you move away from each other.

3) The unmistakable feeling that you've been together before. This comes as a "clicking feeling" as if the missing piece of a puzzle has just been put in place, or a magic key has been turned in a keyhole and the lock "clicks" open. When one of you mentions a past experience that you did not share in this lifetime – you both understand what the other is saying. There is no thinking or analyzing involved; the feelings are strong and knowing.

Our experiences and feelings flow eternally. It's the circumstances that change from lifetime to lifetime, re-entering your life when you are ready to learn something (and sometimes when you're not!)

4) Finally, feeling like you are two halves of a whole. You can

achieve this feeling after years of marriage, but in a Twin Soul or a Soulmate relationship, this also, is felt very quickly in the first stages of the relationship. Not that you can't stand on your own, but each energy individually nurtures and supports the other, giving you a feeling of completion. The powerful Soul relationship is a teaching one. Nowhere else can you grow and learn as much as you do with a Twin Soul or Soulmate. This is why the attraction is so potent and so strong.

As I touched the area of Melanie's palm (just below the wrist bracelets of her inactive hand), I could feel her Soul connections, not only with Heidi, but others as well. I reassured her that she was perfectly normal and counseled her to look at her relationship with Heidi as a gift, rather than comparing it to her marriage. She and Heidi would continue their friendship, teaching and supporting one another for as long as necessary. The nature of the relationship would change one day and so would their circumstances. But they would never lose touch with each other, perhaps meeting again in a future life.

Some people have distinctive lines on their palms, which appear parallel to their line of birth. I interpret these lines as Souls coming into existence at the same time as the person whose palm I'm reading. These unusual, yet subtle lines give me insight as to whether you will be meeting up with any Soul people in this lifetime. If the markings are there, the possibility exists. Whether you choose to cultivate this experience or not, is up to you.

How does one truly go about finding his or her Soulmate? The first thing to do is *stop looking*! The worst possible thing you can do is to go out looking for your Soulmate. When you focus too much on and try to force a situation, it doesn't happen. Why this contradiction? Think about it. How do you feel when you are tense, worried, or needy? What messages are you sending out? Are you open and ready to create space for favorable experiences to come into your life, or are you closed up, tense and tight with worry, creating pessimistic experiences?

By focusing on neediness or worrying, you actually create more negative experiences, instead of positive ones. Like planting a seed, then anxiously uncovering it every few hours to see if it is growing yet. Your own growth slows down, actually prolonging your search. As a result, you end up waiting much longer to meet one another. Focus on feeling good about yourself, about deserving a loving, abundant lifestyle. Blend that with an attitude of faith or trust in the universe and.... presto! You are sending out loving, positive messages which in turn, will magnetize loving, positive people and situations to you.

How do we attract lucrative luck? Favorable fortune? Positive people?

1) First, we must create the desire. We must truly want something before it can happen. What the Soul desires is exactly what it needs for its evolution. Otherwise, there would be no stimulus, no drive, no initiative. However, worrying about it, as mentioned earlier, will repel rather than attract.

2) Second, it is important to concentrate on working with energy in order to bring that object or person to us. Guided imagery, affirmations, feeling and living as though we already have what we want, are some examples of the energetic work necessary to create what we desire. Magic spells won't hurt either.

3) Finally, once again, the letting go part, which is often the most difficult. Stop worrying about "what if" and trust that you will get what you need at just the right time in your life. Tall order? You betcha!

Sending our desire out into the Universe and letting go of the outcome is a valuable part of the process. Once the pressure is off and we "forget about it", if it is for our greatest good, then we will receive it; if it is not, we won't. It's as simple as that!

How will you know when you have found your Soulmate? Instant recognition. You just know. How do you know when you are in love? Same thing; you just know. Nothing can compare to those feelings.

Are you really looking for a Soulmate? Sometimes we fool ourselves into believing something that is just not so.

Last week Maya, a roly-poly woman in her early 30's came to see me. Comfy jeans, T-shirt and long sweater adorned her plump figure. She chose to sit in a green chair – the color of the heart chakra. Her reading was going quite well, when out of the blue she asked me a funny question.

"All my friends talk about finding their Soulmate or that they have already found him. It's beginning to get on my nerves. I don't think my husband and I are Soulmates. I don't even know what that really means, or what the fuss is all about. Does that mean we're not meant for each other and we're gonna split up?"

Maya was moving around nervously in her chair, her voice catching in her throat, and I could see that she was quite apprehensive.

"No," I said in a reassuring tone of voice. "If you are happy with your husband that is just fine. You have a beautiful marriage line, so he's a keeper. That's the way it is meant to be for both of you. You don't have to be in a Soulmate relationship to be happy. It just might not be the right experience for you in this lifetime."

"Well, what about children? We don't have any yet, and I thought that maybe because we're not Soulmates, we just can't have any!"

Poor Maya. She had listened to her friends talking about Soulmates, and somehow twisted the idea around to form some kind of explanation as to why she wasn't able to conceive.

"Let's see if you have any Children's Lines, Maya." Picking up her active hand, I zoomed into the area just below her baby finger (Mercury finger). Two bold lines stood out quite clearly, like soldiers at attention. A smaller, more slanted line followed a little further away.

"I hope you are ready for this – you will have 2 strong, sturdy boys very soon. There is also a possibility of a third child, a girl." I stopped, waiting for a reaction.

"Are you sure?" she asked, immediately perking up. Sparkly eyes told me she was pleased.

"Get ready to go shopping for baby clothes! But I must clarify something - the line indicating the birth of a daughter is not a deep, clear line, so I believe that the decision about having a third child will be made a few more years down the road. You and your husband may feel after having two boys, that your family is complete. If that happens, this smaller, more superficial line representing another child, will eventually fade away. If, when the time comes, you do decide to have another child, the line will grow deeper.

Life is full of experiences. Finding your Soulmate is one of many wonderful and exciting experiences we can choose to create, whether it be in this lifetime or another.

Past Lives

Nobody really knows whether we've lived before or if past life readings are accurate. There's no way to be 100% sure. I believe past life readings are meant to help us sort out the problems we encounter today. Time and again when channeling a past life reading for a client, I find a common thread, linking many of their lives together. This thread tells us the theme, or important experiences the Soul needs for its evolution. The challenges, situations and lessons one faces are valuable. Whether the Soul is born to a male or female body, doesn't matter in the long run. However, there are times when the lessons will be more meaningful if the Soul resides in the body of a man – or woman, depending on society or the period in time. Ultimately, it is the evolution of the Soul that keeps us coming back to this wonderful planet we call Earth.

I remember a client of mine who constantly took on other peoples' problems. She came to see me because she was depressed and fed up. I thought it might be appropriate to incorporate a past life reading into her session with me. What we discovered was that all through the ages, whether in the body of a man or woman, this client managed to find herself in the position of being overly responsible for the troubles of others. Family and friends would "dump" on her. By neglecting her needs to care for others, her own body suffered. Her health deteriorated to the point where she could not even look after herself. In many of her lives, she ended up dying at an early age.

As we traveled the labyrinth of her Soul lives, a distinctive pattern began to emerge. It was clear by the end of the reading, that she had been given an opportunity in this life to break that unwholesome pattern and change her karma.

Another client seemed to be fighting her way through life. Every single past life we unearthed, found her leading the life of a warrior. And this time around, she had chosen to study police technology.

Honestly, I did not know what to tell her. She was not in any distress over her life pattern, so perhaps my lack of insight was not much of an issue. Her reason for coming was to accompany a friend. Curious, she decided to partake in a reading of her own.

I treated myself to a past life reading, many years ago, and as with anything else, some of it felt true and some didn't. When something rings true, it resonates or vibrates within. It is usually felt around the area of your heart, although some people feel it a little lower, in the solar plexus area. Others describe this feeling as if a light bulb just snapped on, or a key clicked in a lock; something falling smartly into place. Whatever doesn't fit or feel right is either information that is not accurate (which is why it grates at you like sandpaper), or it is something you are not quite ready to hear. Undoubtedly, it will find you at some point, when you're in a more receptive frame of mind.

Sitting across the table from me was Pat, an older, white-haired gentleman. He had a kindly face and pink aura. We were at the Psychic Fair in Montreal, Canada and I had decided at the end of the day to close my booth early so I could indulge in a past life reading of my own.

Pat took my hands in his, looked through a magnifying glass at the lines, then put it down and began to channel information to me. He told me some wonderfully accurate things about my life. As we went back into my past lives, I became aware of behavior patterns, I must have subconsciously created for my own evolution. Now I understood why during the early part of my life I often felt lonely. Over the duration of several lives, I had been the firstborn, having to take on much responsibility at an early age. There was no one to talk to about feelings in those days. Survival was the way of life and I was inevitably responsible for my younger siblings.

One of the things he advised me to do was learn the ancient skill of pottery making. Apparently, he had seen me as a famous potter in another life, so in his opinion, the act of shaping clay with my hands was an effective technique to connect with those past lives.

Intrigued and willing to try new experiences, I took his advice and arranged to register for a pottery class. Unfortunately, the class was full – complete – no room left for me. Did I listen to my inner voice that said, "This is not for you"? No, of course not. Ignoring my intuition, I pushed. I called the teacher at home. "If anyone drops out of this class, could I please, please, take their place?"

Magically it happened. One of the students changed her plans at the last minute and canceled. Hurray! I had wanted it so badly, that I believe I actually created a spot for myself in that class.

However, once there, I was in for a surprise. It was not at all what I expected. It was frustrating! No, I couldn't make beautiful vases the first day – or even after lots of practice! The pottery wheels were uncomfortable, the clay slippery and even if I managed to shape something that vaguely resembled a vase or pot, it wouldn't stay put! It wobbled out of shape and then collapsed. I soon found out that pottery requires a lot of skill and patience, and I was *not* naturally gifted in this area. Famous potter – ha! I think not!

As well, because of my commitment to those pottery classes, I was unable to join a choir that sounded like fun. And, on top of that, an opportunity came along for me to fly off to Florida with a friend for a week in the sun. Unfortunately, it would mean missing the last two pottery classes. So, what did I do? Why, I threw in the towel and off I went.

CHAPTER 7

CREATING PROSPERITY – WILL I GET RICH?

What is abundance? Abundance can refer to a particular lifestyle, our relationships, money in the bank, or happiness. Abundance for one person is the dream of having a roof over his head and food in his stomach every day. To someone else it might be living in a richly furnished castle surrounded by acres of property, or on his own private island with phenomenal sums of money at his fingertips.

To others, rich means having children, a loving family or enjoying good health. However we define abundance it feels good. It means feeling fulfilled, having a positive outlook, or living a favorable lifestyle.

One weekend in April, I was teaching a Prosperity Workshop to a group of ladies for the first time. I started the session off by tossing out a question:

"What does abundance mean to you?"

Expecting people to say: "Money in the bank, a beautiful home, new cars, a castle in Spain, etc." I was in for a surprise.

The room went utterly still. No one spoke.

"Inner peace," Jolene burst out.

"Love," sang Florence reverently.

"Wisdom," chanted Effie.

I looked around. Holy smokes! Were they for real? My heart flopped around in my chest. Now what do I do? There went my whole course preparation down the drain. These were the values that I was supposed to be teaching them that day. And they already knew all the answers! Appearing outwardly calm, I cleared my throat in an attempt to squash my rising panic. What

I really wanted to do was cry, run away, or end the class and go home.

However, I kept my cool, projected an aura of serenity somehow and decided to go with the flow. After some discussion, and deeper delving behind their words, the truth finally dawned on me. They were all covering up! My work, of course, instantly doubled! Before even thinking about the class material I had prepared, I first had to break down their mental and emotional blocks concerning money.

To say I was relieved when that class was over was an under-statement, but I did learn some valuable lessons. Reflecting on that workshop, a while later, I also realized that my greatest learning always comes from teaching others.

A lot of people think of money in terms of good or evil. Too much power is attached to it. A much better way to experience the flow of money, wealth, riches, etc., is to visualize it as a circle of energy constantly swirling. We receive it and we give it away. It flows towards us; it flows away from us. If we can let go of the hold money has over us, we will stop feeling controlled by its power. Once we can relax and allow this energy to flow uninter-rupted, the more abundant we become. If we block the flow through tired, old thought patterns or fear, we block our ability to enjoy the wealth of the Universe.

Having a look to see if you have a "Sun Line" will tell me whether you have the potential to become wealthy (remember that line from Chapter 5 snuggling up to your ring finger?). If you have a deep, fairly straight Sun Line or Finance Line, money should flow easily to you. By loosening up and giving this energy freely and sensibly, (you don't just throw it out the window) more will flow back to you in a circle, allowing the cycle to continue. In contrast, if you grasp on to your money tightly, hoarding it under the floorboards, the energy flow will stop (or the mice will chew it up).

A person who feels worthy of wealth will more easily accept

this energy into their lives than someone who doesn't feel they deserve abundance; whether it be money, love or good health. The person who feels undeserving will subconsciously put up a wall to repel, or send their good fortune back into the Universe because they are not open to receive it. "I always have bad luck," they will lament.

We have the power to co-create our reality. What does this mean? In simple terms – we, along with our Creator, make things happen in our life. Our part of the bargain is to focus on what we want, not what we don't want. Whatever we focus on is what we get, because energy follows thought.

Obviously, there will be times when it doesn't work. We are focusing like mad on something we really want - like taking a trip around the world, or raising elephants in our backyard. It doesn't happen. Life gets in the way. That is where the "co" part of the equation shows its presence.

We are not *so* powerful that we can create our existence all alone. The Universe, God, Goddess, Source, Divine Spirit or whatever you believe is the real creator in life.

However, we are still the other half of the "co", the part we have some control over, so if we direct our energy and thoughts into the wonderful feelings abundance can bring us, the more abundance we will attract into our lives. By radiating our vitality, love, joy, and inner peace, we become the source of our own wealth.

If we focus on what we don't want, or on pessimistic feelings or worries, we will only attract more of the same.

In other words, it is better to focus on "I would love a more fulfilling job," rather than "I really hate this job."

By opening and connecting to the abundance of the Universe (deep breathing is a wonderful technique to enhance the process) we are paving the way towards fulfilling our dreams and wishes. Anything is possible.

Do you enjoy going to work? If not, why are you making

yourself miserable day after day? All of your good energy is being wasted on people you don't need to be around and places you don't want to be in. Why are you sacrificing yourself in this way?

[4]Eckhart Tolle in his book *The Power Of Now* says "if you don't like a situation, there are 3 things you can do:

1) leave the situation
2) change the situation
3) accept it

Let's suppose you can't leave your job for economic reasons, and you don't want to accept things the way they are. There is one solution left – to change the situation you are uncomfortable with.

The process starts with changing your mind – actually, your attitude. Instead of concentrating on how unhappy you are, try focusing on the positive aspects of your job. Is it close to home? Do you have friendly co-workers? Is the pay good in spite of the fact that you don't like the work? With this tiny shift in perspective, you should feel a little more optimistic about yourself, and your ability to make changes.

Next, make a point of spending some time playing. Relax and have fun. Leave those "bad vibes" at work. Sing, dance, garden, go out to dinner, socialize, play tennis, make love, express yourself in satisfying ways.

Can you see what is happening? Slowly and gradually you will feel this tiny shift beginning to take on momentum; moving away from your negative thought patterns, towards more positive ones. With a bit of patience and consistency (it won't work in a day or two), you will find yourself creating the changes that you desire. The law of attraction will magnetize or encourage, if you will, more positive experiences – making that promotion, raise, or transfer to a more stimulating department a reality instead of a wish. If you are determined to focus on how horrible this job is and you can't possibly quit, then your negative energy will attract more of the same conditions.

If you're still not convinced, think about this: Walk into a Tim Horton's coffee shop. The Solicitous Server greets you immediately, with a big smile and a friendly, "How are you today?" Well, actually, you were rather preoccupied with a personal problem, but tactfully don't say anything. You place your order. She chats amicably while pouring your coffee from a fresh pot, hands you the cup, and offers you a free sample of their newest doughnuts. You accept, responding with a smile to Solicitous, and leave her a tip – which you hadn't planned on. It wasn't the doughnut sample – good grief, you can buy yourself a doughnut any time you feel like it. It was the server's cheerful mood, friendliness and positive aura that you responded to. You leave the shop with a smile on your face, feeling better than when you first walked in.

Let's contrast that with the same scenario, different server. You stroll into Tim Horton's in a happy mood; after all, this is payday! Solicitous is off today so Slovenly is behind the counter. Slovenly Server ignores you, even though you are standing patiently at the counter waiting for your coffee. There are some stale-looking doughnut pieces put out carelessly on a plate for customers to sample (at their own risk). You clear your throat, or perhaps say "excuse me". She looks over at you and continues cleaning the coffee pots. Becoming impatient, you bang your purse or wallet on the counter, clear your throat a few more times and glance around the room for sympathy from other customers. No one pays attention to you. They are all munching doughnuts or leisurely sipping their own coffee.

Turning back to the counter, you prepare to say something rude or walk away, when with a theatrical sigh, Slovenly server puts down her dishcloth and lifts her eyebrows in your direction. You give her your order. She dumps the coffee from the bottom of the pot – yuk! Into your cup. "Excuse me, do you have a fresh pot brewing? I don't like the coffee at the bottom of the pot. It's too strong." She glares at you as if you've just cut her off in your car or splashed her from head to toe with muddy rainwater. With a grunt of disgust, she splats the coffee down the sink, pours a fresh one and puts her hand out for the money. You pay. No tip. As you leave the coffee shop you wonder what happened to your good mood.

A bright young fellow came to see me. He chose to sit (or rather hunch) in a lemon yellow chair. Considering his age, I felt this was appropriate. Yellow is the color of the solar plexus chakra – the "me" center, the identity center. Dirty blond hair hung down his slumped shoulders and his normally shiny brown eyes were troubled. His problems were written all over his face and extended into his aura. I didn't really need to look at his palm to figure out what was wrong.

Mark needed to find work desperately to pay for his college education. He was so worried about finances that he was having trouble concentrating on his studies.

"Do what you love to do and then find out how to get paid for it," I suggested. After a moment of thought, he looked up at me.

"Well, I love to spend time kayaking, but what good is that going to do me?"

Taking his palm in my hand, I noticed that he had a strong Jupiter finger, the sign of a "take charge" person.

"Mark, why don't you start up a kayak program at school?" I asked.

"A what?"

"A program where students are taught the basics of kayaking. You could organize wilderness trips, if that appeals to you, or learn the skill of building your own kayak. You could hold kayak-building workshops in the summertime."

I paused for a moment to allow this information to sink in. "And while we're at it, we might as well see what your numbers tell us, Mark. What is your date of birth?"

"May 7, 1978," he answered promptly.

"Hmmm, that adds up to a 37, which reduces to a single number of 1. One is the number of a leader, a magician, a pathfinder. Perfect for breaking new ground or initiating new programs. If there is a way to make money, you will find it. The 3 represents creative expression and the 7 imagination and sensitivity. You seem to have the right combination of birth path numbers to create fun, travel, new avenues of expression and eventually – wealth."

I could sense the excitement starting to build in him as he absorbed this new information. "Wow that sounds awesome!" He exclaimed, his face lighting up.

Feeling that he really wasn't interested in the rest of the reading, I cut it short. Mark was anxious to get home and get moving on his new project.

A common belief people share is thinking that having large sums of money or material possessions will fill their inner needs. Take a few moments to contemplate what inner quality(s) you feel having lots of money will bring to you. If you think having more money will give you confidence in yourself, then confidence or self-esteem is the very quality you need to develop in order to draw money to you. If you think you will have more freedom, more friends, more fun, or feel more alive by gathering stacks of money, then begin to imagine that you already have those traits.

By feeling as if you already have what you need, your energy will change to fit in with your desires. It may take some time. Change often does. Once you get to the point where you do feel more confident or develop more strength or enjoy personal freedom, then you become magnetic to the money you desire. In other words, turn your thoughts around. Instead of saying to yourself:

"If only I had more money, I would be a confident (fun, courageous, popular) person."

Change that to:

"Once I learn to develop self-confidence (self-esteem, courage, poise, strength, etc.), I will automatically draw more money to me."

Sounds too easy? Think it won't work for you? Get rid of that negative thought **right now**! Whatever is meant to be for your own good, will flow to you when the time is right. The world in its natural state is uncomplicated. We are the ones who make things complicated.

Let's go back to those inner qualities or areas in our lives that need some work – the ones that are holding us back from success, whether personally or in business. Think about it for a moment. Rather than *needing* money to fill a lack, or to "fix" what we feel is holding us back, turn it around the other way.

Use the process of creating money and material possessions as a tool to help you develop greater self-esteem, confidence and freedom, so you can more fully express yourself. Self-expression is the key to your soul's purpose (more about that later).

Do you think being wealthy will give you a greater sense of personal power, more freedom or will make you feel more alive?

All by itself it won't. There are plenty of rich people who take orders from others, denying their own self-expression, identity and soul's purpose. Their wealthy lifestyle has them trapped in a cage. They are expected to behave in a certain manner, dress to conform to society's code and even eat and drink what someone else dictates.

Not everyone who is wealthy lives this way, of course. The focal point in this example is to understand that developing and expressing your own personal power is your pathway to success. Hoarding your gold like Ebenezer Scrooge just won't do it.

Once you've reached that point where you feel in tune with (and not frightened of) your own power, and are confident enough to express or radiate that inner quality – then you become more attractive to wealth. Living your life through someone else's eyes or trying to measure up to someone's expectations of you, no matter how noble, is not the pathway to success. Your personal power will not shine. Your aura will be cloudy, pushing success just out of reach.

Accept the challenge and turn your life around. Your potential is written in your palms; your future is in your very own hands.

YOU have the power to create your world any way you want it. Are you ready?

CHAPTER 8

YOUR SOUL PURPOSE

What are you doing here? Do you have a soul purpose? Does everyone? What is a soul purpose?

As time goes on, we, who are living in this day and age want more out of life. We are not satisfied with the kind of life our parents and grandparents lived. We've learned how to meditate, to transform our energy, to access our "higher self", and now we are curious; wishing to explore our soul's desire, soulmates, and our "soul purpose". Reaching beyond the purely physical world to delve into the spiritual realm is becoming a way of life, now more widely accepted as we've entered a new millennium, the Age of Aquarius. What does it mean? How is "soul purpose" different from "life purpose?"

Life purpose is associated with a job, career, what you are accomplishing in this life – like mother, jeweler, scuba diver, snake breeder, etc. It may or may not be connected to soul purpose, changing according to life's phases of growth and evolution. Soul purpose goes a little deeper. It is more descriptive of you as a person, *being*, rather than *doing*.

People today are less satisfied with superficial explanations than they were in the past. We want to find answers. We need to dig deep down to the roots of our issues. We want to feel fulfilled. Some of us decide to take the route into our past lives for answers to problems today.

Alexandra came to me for a past life reading. Brought up by the sea, yet terrified of water, she felt strange and out of place at home. Her parents found it very trying that little Alex didn't want to go anywhere near the water. Their other children naturally took to water at an early age, living for the sole (soul?) purpose of swimming, diving and fishing. Alexandra told me she felt like an outcast, like she didn't fit in. As I tuned into her energy field, a flow of pictures swirled across my intuition screen. One scene in particular swooped down, demanding my full attention.

I immediately focused on a clear stream of swiftly running water, flowing beside what looked like a mill, a windmill or gristmill or something. Two little girls, coarsely dressed, but with bright red scarves over their heads, were running and tumbling merrily beside the stream. They were happy and at play. I could tell from their clothing that they were in Europe, perhaps somewhere in the Netherlands. I had no idea what the year was, but intuitively felt that this was long, long ago. The grass was quite high and dry in places, and beyond the stream I could see a dense forest. There were no flowers in sight. I could only guess at the season – early fall, I think.

As the girls ran behind the windmill, the picture faded out. I saw nothing more, but had the distinct feeling that the path between the mill and the stream was very narrow, probably slippery and unsafe. I felt a stab of panic, like a sharp intake of breath, followed by – nothing; just an emptiness, which I interpreted to mean that one or both of the girls had fallen into the stream.

Whether it was a comfort to Alexandra or not, I believe that she was one of those little girls who had drowned in the stream. This fear of water had followed her from one life to another. And now she needed to deal with it. With the answer to her "irrational fear" out in the open, she could start to work on letting it go, and ultimately, move on with her life. She was no longer "stuck" – struggling with her true self as opposed to whom she thought she should be. Her expression of self was no longer clouded in fear. No longer did she feel like an outcast in her homeland – even within the circle of her family. As her false self slipped away, a new Alexandra boldly stepped forward to take her place, and in that process, her true soul began to unfold, like the glistening wings of a butterfly, as it emerges from its cocoon.

Back to soul purpose – very simply put, I believe that your "soul purpose" is to be – just be – be yourself, and express that being. The secret here is to "express". To be able to express your true self (the real person deep down inside), is to be in tune with your soul. I know it is not always easy. Fear of criticism or judgment gets in the way and crushes our expressive little beings. Blessed are those who feel good enough, confidant enough, grounded enough to be themselves.

Soul purpose means allowing your inner person to come out and play. If you reveal the essence of yourself to those around you – family, friends, co-workers and community, they in turn will be encouraged to do the same. When you feel really comfortable letting that inner person out – then you are well on your way to achieving your soul purpose.

Let's dive a little deeper to get a clearer understanding of your reason for being. Where in your personal cycle of life are you? Are you struggling with survival issues, spiritual issues, moral issues, love and relationship issues?

Life is constantly throwing challenges, situations, and monkey wrenches our way for the evolution of our soul. Within the midst of these challenges – poverty, disease, childbirth, marriage, success, failure, your soul must find its oasis of peace.

Continuing to express yourself when surrounded by chaos, is the true meaning of soul purpose. If you want an extreme example of someone who achieved true soul purpose, think of Mother Teresa. Yes, there was a job to do, but the direction came from within, the guidance from above. Her life's work was more an expression of soul than a series of tasks.

If you are looking for guidance to help uncover the mystery of your soul's expression, you might want to pick up a tarot deck – or check out your birth numbers via numerology. As we did with Gaby and Mark (and a few others), adding up your date of birth will give you a number, which is then reduced to a single digit. As mentioned in chapter 2, each number carries a vibration with an associated interpretation or meaning.

If your date of birth reduces to a 5, for instance, the interpretation is one of communication. In other words, the 5 energy belongs to someone who makes communication their life's work. They may be a writer, news broadcaster, journalist, actor or linguist.

In the tarot, the number 5 is the Hierophant. This card represents learning with experts, conforming or identifying with a group. So if you are a number 5, your soul purpose would be through higher learning and communication of this exceptional knowledge, being committed to a cause, and working as part of a team.

Number 9 birth path is the way of the humanitarian; a gentle soul who wishes to save the world. The number 9 in the tarot is the Hermit, the Sage or spiritual guide, who holds up his lantern for others to follow. He leads through example, not by force. The soul purpose of a 9 vibration, is thus geared towards the environment, saving the planet and serving his fellow man.

Soul purpose is not the same as your career or your role in society. It is an expression of your true self. How hard can that be? Well, let me tell you…..

I grew up in an environment where self-expression was regarded as frivolous. It got in the way of the serious business of life. One had to go to school, help with household chores, babysit younger siblings, and plan well ahead for the future. Certainly there was time for play, but as far as expressing the self, giving an opinion, or taking art lessons or ballet, it just wasn't deemed necessary. So, I was swallowed up in the vast crowd of school children (don't forget those were the baby boomer years). High school was just another "conforming" experience. I rarely raised my hand in class to give an answer, preferring to be seen and not heard, or even worse – to make a mistake! Expressing yourself meant behaving differently from the "in-crowd" and was just not done – definitely not cool.

Soul purpose? Are you nuts? Soul stuff was for church, if you went at all.

Today, people and attitudes have changed dramatically. There comes a point in time when we begin to question what we are doing here. We sense that there is a deeper reality to our lives and begin to search for it. Soul purpose is one way of accessing that deeper reality. It gives meaning to our lives, because one of the greatest fears at middle age is – that life is slipping away.

On reaching "middle age" we look back over the early years. Our existence then was filled with activity: "doing, doing, doing". We struggled to balance our working lives with our home lives. We tackled Day Care and job responsibilities. We devoted ourselves to our families, our elders, and even our pets. Juggling became a way of life as we raced against the clock. Life became one great big roller coaster ride. What would it be like to step off? (or fall off, as some of us did). We couldn't even begin to imagine.

Oh, to have a teensy, weensy bit of time – just for us. No one to account to, no one demanding something from us. Just our own time.

Then one day, we finally did get off this roller coaster. Our children grew up and moved away from home. Our parents no longer needed us. Finally, finally we could retire from the rat race. Oh bliss! Pure heaven! The pace of life suddenly slowed; we could savor the quiet, some precious time to ourselves. We could smell the roses without worrying about weeding, or take a quiet walk in the woods. Go on a holiday.

Then what? With the outer activity gone, there is no where to turn but inward. It is time now to face our internal selves; the part of us that's been hiding. The feeling is so strange, so unfamiliar, that frantically we try to keep busy, struggling to fill the void. Do we *really* want back on that roller coaster? Not a chance! But after a while these activities become routine and we can't escape.

It can't be put off any longer. It's time to come face to face with reality. Time to embrace our inner being - and discover who we really are.

Everyone has a variation of this story. Some people have more time to themselves at the beginning of their lives, others at the end and still others in the middle, not realizing that they are in the eye of the storm with more to come! Of course there are those fortunate, confident people who know exactly who they are and what their place is in the world – I haven't met too many, have you?

Once we enter this period of our lives when the outer noise and activity quiet down, we are presented with a golden opportunity to take a closer look at who we really are. Endless hours spent on the job, varied social obligations and functions do not express our true selves.

So, where do we go for help? How do we find some answers?

Bonnie came for a reading recently. "I'm at a crossroads," she told me candidly, her china blue eyes scanning my body in a quick appraisal. I must have passed inspection, because she continued: "I feel lost. My children have moved out and now the house is empty. I feel like I'm not important any more. I was always doing things for my children. Their needs were a priority. But now that they've moved out, there's a hole in my life."

"Oh?" I encouraged. Now it was my turn to scan *her* body. What you see is what you get was my instant assessment. "Sit down, Bonnie."

"I don't know… just thinking about what *I* want for a change makes me feel strange – as if I shouldn't be doing anything just for me. What if I decide to go back to school? That costs money, and if my children need money for something important…" She gave a shrug to her shoulders as if discouraged; then looked away.

"Bonnie, please have a seat," I encouraged, wondering why

she was still standing there, as if not quite sure of herself or me.

"And as if that isn't enough, I started working part-time in a hospital. At first I felt useful, but now it's the same thing, day after day. Everywhere I turn, I feel like a failure! What's my purpose here? Where do I belong?" At this point she plopped down on a red chair, stood up, chose a green chair instead, got up once more and finally sat in a grey chair – all in the space of a few seconds.

Picking up her refined looking hand, I noticed that Bonnie had long, delicate fingers. "Do you ever express yourself artistically?" I asked.

She gave me a funny look, took a few minutes to think and then replied, "I tried sculpture once, but hated it. Painting was frustrating and oh yes!" (she let out a little cry as a new memory flashed across her face). "Music!" Nodding her head vigorously, she reminisced, "I loved to play the piano when I was a little girl. But when my mother died, our piano was sold along with the house and I never played again."

"Why don't you start playing the piano once more," I suggested gently. "It's a beginning. Once you open the door to your own creativity, the rest will flow naturally. You will discover skills or gifts that you never knew you had."

"Like what?" she inquired, leaning forward, clearly intrigued. "Well," I continued, picking up her hand again. "The shape and size of your thumb tells me that you have a strong work ethic. Combined with your long fingers and love of music, you could give piano lessons to children. Or, you could decorate homes or offices, or office homes." She giggled.

"I meant home offices." I giggled too.

"A lot of people work from their homes and might welcome a professional touch, I resumed in what I hoped was a "professional tone", rather than a giggly one. Have you ever thought about feng shui, or healing through color or sound therapy? Your Head Line slopes downward, indicating a good imagination and people skills. You also have the beginnings of Healing Stigmata just under your little finger. Lines change as we change and if you lean towards the healing arts, your healing stigmata will grow stronger. Don't think about becoming a massage therapist, however. Your hands are not that strong."

"Whoa – slow down! You're making my head spin!" she interrupted sitting on both hands. I had no trouble interpreting that kind of body language. Oops, time to put the stopper on my errant Intuition before it bubbles up all over the place, I thought to myself.

"OK, let's back up a bit. Since you come from a musical background, teaching piano would be an excellent way to put those talents to work again. You enjoyed your piano days, why not encourage others to learn? You don't have to restrict yourself to children if you don't want to. There are plenty of adults who are interested in learning to play piano, whether they are just beginners or hope to pick up where they left off years ago.

Teaching is a challenging profession, forcing you to broaden your horizons and better your own skills, in order to pass them on to others."

She chewed on her lip and waited for me to go on.

"With those long, creative fingers," I continued, "you don't need to confine yourself to music. Changing the appearance of home or office space for clients who are looking for something beyond the traditional decorating, would be right up your alley. The stimulation of meeting with people on a regular basis, and working in tandem will certainly fill that empty nest void. Your creative talents will bloom and you'll have fun too! Do you know what feng shui is?"

"Sort of." I took that to mean "no", so I plunged ahead.

"Feng shui is the ancient art of placement, where furniture and decorative items are properly placed within the home (or office) to allow maximum flow of Chi. Chi simply means life force. So, to maximize Chi or life force, one wouldn't put a dining table right smack in front of the entrance door. It blocks the Chi from flowing into the house. You wouldn't have both front and back doors open at the same time, either, because the good Chi would enter through the front door and exit through the back.

"If you want to reflect good Chi in a room, hang mirrors on the wall. It keeps the Chi from leaving the room and the house. Are you beginning to get the picture?"

"I am, and it sounds interesting."

"Feng shui is far more complex than what we've just discussed, but you can check out the internet or take a trip to your favorite book store to learn more.

"What kind of work are you doing in the hospital?" I asked, slowing things down a little.

"I work as an aide and find the job has become routine. I thought I'd love looking after people. I've done it all my life, but somehow it's not working. I don't feel like I'm making any difference in their lives."

"I understand. Once you stop learning or the job loses its challenge, it's time to move on." I smiled at her. "Let's see what else we can uncover." Weaving a little numerology into her reading, I asked for her birth date.

"Your date of birth adds up to a 3", I told her. "Three's are very creative people. They love beauty and need harmonious surroundings and relationships to be happy. Now that we know a little bit more about you, how do you feel?"

"Well," she answered cautiously. "A little overwhelmed, but you've given me lots to think about. I feel better now knowing that there are exciting things for me to explore in the next little while. As to my place in this lifetime, my soul purpose, I don't know yet, but if I can learn something new, and have fun, without taking away from anyone else, or feeling guilty about it – it's a start!"

And how about the younger crowd? The sweet young things coming to me asking about soul purpose? They have barely begun their lives and already are searching for a purpose.

"I want to take over the business," declared Sandy, a skinny raven-haired girl with chewed up fingernails. She worked as a waitress in a bar. "But, I also like hiking, painting, nature studies and languages. I never want to get married or have children. So what would my soul purpose be?"

Taking her hand in mine while sensing her aura, I offered this advice: "Sandy, soul purpose is more an expression of your inner being. If you feel that a business venture or communicating through the study of different languages expresses your true essence, then by all means go for it.

On the other hand, you might not be comfortable at all expressing yourself through these professions or lifestyles. Your soul purpose will naturally unfold as you learn to be yourself. It is important not to be influenced too much by other peoples' opinions. Do what makes you happy. Do what you feel in tune with. You may be very happy working in a shop or a post-office or a car wash. The jobs are self-explanatory; the expression of soul is through service. Or, you may end up expressing yourself through the arts, as a famous dancer, or a not-so-famous cartoonist. It doesn't really matter which form of expression you choose. You will know by the signals your body is giving you what is appropriate for you."

Soul purpose is the big picture. It is the golden thread that weaves itself into the fabric of your activities, your creative and expressive self, your loving self, your relationships. Everything you do has a purpose; everything you feel is for a reason. Honor yourself by allowing your life to unfold the way it was meant to be. Just know in your heart that your life is not meant to be wasted, however simple or complex it is.

CHAPTER 9

OUR FUTURE

Do Babies Have Lines on Their Palms?

A while ago I became a Grandmother. I can hardly believe it! Just the word grandma conjures up visions of little old ladies, gray-haired and crotchety, knitting by the fire while their rocking chairs creak. Well, I guess times are a-changing! This Grandma has only a few gray hairs (really!) She has no idea how to knit, has spider webs draping the arms of her rocking chair and swims, hikes, rides bikes and runs around all summer in tank tops and jean-shorts.

Yes, times are a-changing (now I'm really beginning to sound like a grandmother!) The last time *I* gave birth was more than 25 years ago, so you can imagine my surprise at all the changes surrounding this wondrous event.

The Maternity Ward was located on the third floor of this hospital, so I found the stairs and ran all the way up (well, most of the way). My logical brain told me that I had oodles of time, but my emotional side refused to listen. I was too keyed up with excitement. I burst through the glass doors to the Nursing Station, huffing and puffing looking ridiculous, instead of like the stately grandmother I was supposed to be.

An unruffled, very professional-looking nurse, complete with starched, white cap, was sitting behind the desk, making notations on what looked like (reading upside down) my daughter-in-law's chart.

"Oh!" I squeaked excitedly pointing to the chart. She looked up and spoke one word in a calm tone of voice. "Relationship?"

"Mother," I responded thinking about my son who-was-too-young-to-become-a-father.

With a patient sigh, she looked me up and down and said, "Relationship to the baby." (You dope, she must have been thinking you don't look pregnant or young enough to be the mother.)

"Oh!" I blurted out, embarrassed, "Grandmother!"

"Are you sure?" She peered down her nose through nurse spectacles at me.

Now what? I thought. Not sure whether she was teasing me, flattering me or putting me through some kind of test, I decided to leave well enough alone and just nod. This grandmother thing is going to take a while to get used to!

"Go straight down the hall, turn right and the second door on your left will be Birthing Room 6." Flashing a bright thank-you smile I started down the hall towards the Birthing Rooms (at a more subdued grandmotherly pace, of course.) Turning the corner, I came upon a row of Birthing Room Doors, which were clearly marked not only with individual numbers, but also with delightful bunches of brightly-colored dried flowers. Stopping for a moment to gather my wits, I realized that I was about to open the door to the actual "Place-Where-Mother-Gave-Birth!" Goodness!

In *my day* no one was allowed in the delivery room. Just doctors and nurses, gloved, gowned and masked. Everything was sterile, and family was absolutely forbidden to enter the inner sanctum.

Father was the only one allowed to enter the labor room in those days, where Mother was installed to begin the birth process. The antiseptic labor rooms of yesterday were drab and smelled like a hospital – a place for sick people, not a place for birthing brand new babies! There certainly weren't any frivolous flowers garnishing the door (in fact, I don't even remember a door. It seems like hospital personnel walked in and out as they pleased, while I sweated and groaned, wishing it would hurry up and be over).

After what felt like an eternity, Mom was shunted down the hall to the delivery room, where she was heaved onto a cold, hard, sterile table to finally give birth.

All this zoomed through my head in a flash, as I was preparing to open the door to Birthing Room 6. I knocked quickly and pushed open the door. A surprisingly warm and inviting atmosphere greeted me - not scary at all! Looking around, I noticed color and comfort, not bedpans and thermometers. I was totally captivated by the soft, rose-colored walls and appealing dried flower arrangements. Tastefully matching window curtains complimented the décor. I felt like I'd taken a wrong turn and walked into Decorator's Dream!

There was no end to the contrast; the tremendous change from sterile and institutional, to this warm, happy, friendly family-oriented place. This room felt about as far away from a cold, impersonal hospital room as I could ever imagine.

The air was crackling with excitement, as the whole family gathered around "the couple" about to give birth. A radio played soothing background music that nobody was listening to, and a television sat neglected in a corner, ready to turn on if anyone got bored while waiting for "Baby" to arrive.

And "Baby" did arrive – a beautifully formed pink little girl. Mom and Dad were overwhelmed and exhausted with the whole procedure of giving birth, but the Grandmas were exhilarated – we'd already had our turn years ago and thankfully didn't have to go through that again!

Finally, it was my turn to hold this brand-new life in my arms. What an incredible feeling! My heart filled with wonder and love for this perfect little baby – and I didn't have to go through one single labor pain!

"Mom?" Tearing my eyes away from the newborn little bundle who was Jessica, I looked up into the gentle brown eyes of my son – the young father.

"Mom?" he repeated, "will you read Jessica's palm?" Read Jessica's palm! Wow! A tidal wave of emotion surged through me as a million thoughts swam through my brain. But, she's less than an hour old, what could I possibly see in this teeny tiny newborn hand? Suddenly, I panicked. What if she did not have any lines? Looking around the room, I noticed everyone was waiting expectantly for me to say something.

"Sure," I replied calmly, as if I do this every day of my life. Looking first at Jessica's mother who nodded her approval (she was probably too tired to care) I slowly and gently uncurled each pink little finger. What would I do if she really had no lines? What would I see? Would both hands be the same? How could I read her past? She doesn't have one yet. When I finally uncurled Jessica's fragile little fist, to my surprise I saw that she had lots of lines! Quickly uncurling her other hand, I discovered that indeed, both hands appeared to be the same. And then I lost myself in reading this brand new little person.

Why read babies and small children at all? They change and grow so rapidly, is it really worth it? Some mothers are curious, some genuinely interested. Personally, I find reading a baby's palm exciting. It's like opening a Christmas present! Will he or she be strong, determined, goal-oriented? Or blossom into a creative soul, gentle and musically inclined? Will he make friends easily or need help? Is he gifted? Will she excel in sports? Or is it better to encourage an academic lifestyle? What about past lives? How will they influence this one?

Yes, their lines will change as they grow, but this "sneak preview" is enough to give Mom and Dad a privileged glimpse into the years ahead, as they guide their offspring through the maze of life towards happiness and success.

Bradley, my sister's four-year-old son has a Simian Line on his Left Hand. A Simian line is the joining together of the Head and Heart Lines to form one single line (straight across the palm). This line is quite distinct. You will see it frequently on people born with Down syndrome, usually on both hands. Interestingly, this same line can also be seen on individuals who possess a high level of intelligence. From one extreme to another, they share a common trait, however - single-mindedness and tenacity. Because of their love of nature and animals, you will find them enjoying careers as environmentalists, park rangers, agricultur-alists, and animal trainers. These "down-to-earth" people represent the beginning of our evolution. Methodical, loyal, and good with their hands, they are often instinctively in survival mode.

"Watch out!" I told my sister over coffee one afternoon, about a month after my granddaughter's birth. "Bradley is a power-house of energy." She rolled her eyes at me in exasperation.

"I certainly don't need you to tell me that! I live with him every day, remember?" sarcasm dripped from her voice.

"Seriously," I went on with a smile on my face, choosing to ignore this playful sisterly exchange. "Because of this rare line on his left palm, we know that everything he sets out to accomplish, he does with intensity. There are no half measures. Fortunately, this Simian Line is in his left hand (his inactive one) so he will be able to balance his intense energy with periods of downtime when he needs to. If it were in his right hand, then you would have a tougher job. His right hand is the active one – the one foretelling the future. That means, the qualities of this line would become more pronounced with time; he would tend to see issues in black or white only, no shades of gray or very little compromise.

"Your job," I continued, "is to channel his excessive energy positively, so he doesn't use it to get into too much mischief. Provide him with a means of release – lots of interesting and varied activities, for instance, so he doesn't turn that energetic geyser into destructive behavior. By starting now, you will be paving a happier more constructive pathway for him to follow throughout his life. Add a touch of coyote medicine, and you will be able to redirect troublesome behavior and pent-up energy as he grows up."

"Coyote medicine?"

"Yes, you know, being sneaky."

"What?"

"Oh come on, you know what I'm talking about; incorporating the good-for-you things into food or activities they already like, so they don't notice it."

"Like what?"

"Oh, you could try giving him Superman toothpaste so he will *want* to brush his teeth. Or slipping yukky-tasting medicine into his chocolate milk. All mothers use coyote medicine."

"Gottcha."

"But as far as re-directing his energy, you may have to enroll him in hockey, soccer *and* baseball - not one or the other."

The rest of Brad's palm shows very few lines. A rather uncomplicated individual, he will grow up to be a man of action – strong and determined. Nothing will stand in his way. He is a "doer" and consequently will use relatively few words to get what he wants.

His one-year-old sister, however, has many many lines covering her tiny palms. Sarah is an old, old spirit, having lived many previous lives. She holds in her hands the wisdom of the ages. She will be far more flexible and tactful than her brother, using subtle and diplomatic methods to get the results she wants.

"Thanks for the info, sis. Now I can push them in the right direction."

"Guide them," I corrected gently, with my newfound grandmother's wisdom.

I happened to be in Chinatown a couple of summers ago with friends, when I was introduced to Michelle. Michelle, a motherly-looking young woman was sitting comfortably on a bench cuddling her four-month old son. Gently, I reached for her baby's hand. The little one smiled and gurgled, totally unaware that he was granting me the privilege of unfolding and deciphering his map; the tiny map in his palm that told of the journey he was just beginning in this life. Voices and people around me faded out, as I became totally absorbed in reading this little boy. "Wait!" interrupted his mother breaking my concentration. "Would you mind if I videotaped this? I'd like him to see it when he is older and able to understand. Would you please start over?" So I did.

Our young – they hold the future in their hands like tiny flower buds slowly unfolding. What will they do with their world? How have we taught and shaped them to cope and live in this New Age, this new millennium?

Final Words of Wisdom

Laura came to see me the other day. "Come in and sit down," I welcomed her. She followed me to my healing room and settled herself in a comfortable chair. Scented candles glowed softly in the evening dusk, while tea lights flickered from my lava rock waterfall, which I had set on a low table to enhance the atmosphere. I could feel excitement bubbling out of her as she tried to appear calm. "Herbal tea?" I offered. "Oh yes, please," she giggled.

Laura was an aesthetician. Twenty-two years old, a little shy, but filled with a typical young girl's hopes and dreams. Shiny dark brown hair swung around her shoulders and her eyes were glowing with anticipation. She asked the usual questions about her love life, marriage, her career, family and friends and then came the question I had been dreading – "How many children will I have?"

Kate was frightened. A middle-aged woman with health issues, she came to me hoping I would tell her that she would live a full, normal lifespan. Fearing the worst, she needed to hear something positive, something to hope for. Carefully applied make-up, warm earthy-toned skirt, cream-coloured blouse and matching fashionable shoes, gave one the impression that she was just fine.

Claire and Danny came to see me. She had stars in her eyes and love in her heart. Danny was a little restless. That he cared for her was obvious, but I doubted if he was in love.

"Oh, it looks like you'll be moving." I caught myself just in time. Telling him that he was going to move, when I didn't see a move in her hand was not the right thing to say. "But not for a while," I amended, hoping that I had repaired the damage.

Wouldn't you know – two months later, Claire called me to say that they were having trouble in their relationship and what was it I said about Danny moving?

Have you found the common denominator in these situations? How does one become the bearer of bad news? How do I tell that excited, eager young girl that she will not have children, when she so obviously longs to be a mother one day? By planting that kind of seed in her mind, I'd be casting a shadow over her upcoming marriage. Suppose depression set in, and she decided not to get married at all, depriving herself of a natural, loving, joyous life. Or, she could decide to place the blame on her lover; and in the process destroy a beautiful relationship. On top of that, denying the truth is not the way to solve a problem. It will still be there when she finds another man.

What if I don't tell her the truth? Suppose I lie a little and tell her she will have a couple of cute, healthy children one day. After all "one day" is far, far away. Well, deception is just not my style. I couldn't live with myself if I practiced deception. And, with the passage of time, she would either get conflicting advice from other readers, or become frustrated trying to conceive and forgo adoption because she listened to and believed in me.

Some people unwittingly help me out. If I say to them "It looks like you may not be having children." They will say "Good, I have no time for babies." Those are the easiest to deal with. What I had perceived as a potential problem, is not a problem at all. In fact, it is just the way they wish their life to be.

Then there are the stubborn ones who try to force me with their energy. They want an answer and they want it now! I can feel that energy force as if they were pushing me physically, and in reaction, I put up a wall. This invisible wall is meant to protect; to protect my clients from suddenly hearing painful news, and to caution me to slow down. With as much tact as possible, I will find a way to let them know what lies ahead on their chosen path.

Strangely enough, those people who have pushed for an answer don't really listen to what I have to say. Either they don't believe me, or are not receptive at all. They have a one-track mind and will listen only if I agree. So, what do I tell them?

How do I tell Kate that she has only a few years left on this earth? Is it really my place to make that kind of prediction? Suppose I'm wrong? After all, I am human and will make mistakes. And, medical science being what it is – you never know when a cure or break-through will be found. The timing might be perfect for her – or it might not.

How do I tell that sweet young couple that they will not last beyond the end of the year? How do I shatter hopes and dreams? What possible good comes from telling people bad news – news that they don't want to hear anyway?

On the other hand – they did come for a reading. They did come for guidance. They did come for honesty - or did they? What kind of a reader/healer would I be if I closed my eyes to the truth and blithely told them that everything would be all right, knowing that a break-up was imminent? How honest is that?

Who am I to assume that people are not capable of handling the problems life throws at them? Who am I to assume that my clients are not able to face challenges designed to help them grow? There is a fine line between giving someone hope and placating them. There is a fine line between honesty and bluntly stating bad news. Delicate matters must be handled with care. It is the sensitive Palm Reader who learns to walk that fine line without falling off, to distinguish between true guidance and "taking the easy way out". Where does hope and guidance begin and deception end?

Remember Pat, that kindly, white-haired gentleman (from Chapter 6), who gave me a past-life reading? Well, he started off my reading by switching off the tape recorder and saying "There is a possibility for you to have two marriages." Being a sensitive and responsible reader, he was treading with care. "Fine," I answered right away. "I am on my second marriage".

I liked his approach. Rather than egotistically stating that I will have two marriages because that's what is in my hand does nothing but give the reader a misplaced sense of power over the client. Pointing out the *possibility* for a situation or set of circumstances will get the message across, while shifting the power back to the client where it belongs. They will then be in a position to make their own choices and decisions.

Palm Readers (or any readers for that matter) carry a responsibility to guide – not destroy people. A reliable, trustworthy Palm Reader will recognize the vulnerability of clients, knowing that they will act on information given to them.

Therefore, once you decide to go for a reading, it is important to choose your palmist carefully.

Word of mouth is a good way. It is preferable to choose someone recommended by a trusted friend, taking into account personal differences of course.

It is also important to listen to your palmist and then take only the advice that feels right for you. When an idea or piece of advice feels right, it resonates within you. If anything does not click or gives you an uncomfortable feeling, then it is not right for you.

Do not be afraid to trust your feelings. Learning to trust your feelings or inner voice is an important part of your spiritual growth and development. Discernment is part of that wonderful voyage of self-discovery. Do not take every piece of advice as gospel. Follow your instincts; follow your own drum.

Remember, a palmist is just a guide – not a God.

Footnotes

1   Heal Your Body, Louise Hay, California, Hay House, 1984

2   Palmistry booklet by Peter Keog and Kathleen Keog of the Palmistry Centre, Montreal, Qc, Canada, 1997.

3.   Heal Your Body, Louise Hay, California, Hay House, 1984

4.   The Power of Now, Eckhart Tolle, New World Library, 2004

BOOKS

O is a symbol of the world, of oneness and unity. In different cultures it also means the "eye," symbolizing knowledge and insight. We aim to publish books that are accessible, constructive and that challenge accepted opinion, both that of academia and the "moral majority."

Our books are available in all good English language bookstores worldwide. If you don't see the book on the shelves ask the bookstore to order it for you, quoting the ISBN number and title. Alternatively you can order online (all major online retail sites carry our titles) or contact the distributor in the relevant country, listed on the copyright page.

See our website **www.o-books.net** for a full list of over 500 titles, growing by 100 a year.

And tune in to myspiritradio.com for our book review radio show, hosted by June-Elleni Laine, where you can listen to the authors discussing their books.